child's play

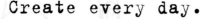

Create every day.

   Collage Unleashed! These are two words that sum up my artistic working style. Here's an insight into my playful and funky art world. I am excited to share with you my mixed-media techniques, and I hope to bring a childlike spirit and playfulness out of you when you are creating art. My adult workshops have been developed from many of the children's art classes that I teach. In this book, you will explore fun techniques such as painting and dying paper and fabric, monoprint sandwiches, freestyle graffiti lettering, doodling, funky embroidery, painting with crayons and more. You will also learn several book binding techniques such as free-form bead macramé, knotted fabric and free-form crochet. These are simple techniques using easy-to-find materials and tools that you can mix in interesting ways to create unique and personal art journals, art quilts, collage and more.

   My vision for this book is to have you feel like you are at one of my workshops, where the spirit of creativity is free-flowing, there are no mistakes and anything goes! The first five chapters of the book are presented in how-to instruction with a combination of inspirational photographs of my artwork and detailed step-by-step instructions, including creative ideas and jump starts. Keep in mind that these techniques are just the beginning, here for you to experiment with, then to take and put your own twist to them. The projects that make up the final chapter are presented as a guide for you to create your own artwork based on my mixed-media techniques. Intertwined within the book pages are lots of doodles and art for you to photocopy and use in your collage work. I want this book to be interactive. Use it as an inspirational workbook: write notes in the margin, add your own doodles and write idea lists. Visit my Web site for additional downloads, inspiration and project information (www.treicdesigns.com). I hope to inspire you to unleash your creativity!

   It's been almost five years since I took the leap from the high-tech world of Silicon Valley to pursue my passion for art full-time. It has been a great adventure, filled with a lot of hard work, minimal sleep, lots of Starbucks, and the desire to do what makes me happy. This journey has taught me that, if you are doing what you love and are passionate about it, everything that you work hard to accomplish will happen. I can truly say that I have found my passion and am happy to be able to share it with you.

   pLaY.dReAm.eXpLorE.cReAtE! Browse my Web site, doodle in your journal, paint colorful stories—do something creative every day! I hope to inspire you with my art.

i am inspired by everything and
everyone
that enters my path.
i find art in everything
and everything finds its way into my art.

play.Dream.

explore.Create.

Contents

dedication

To my family: Daddy, Mom, Dude, Freedom and Trei-Trei.
I am living my dreams. Thank you for your love, support
and encouragement—I love you.

In loving memory: Grandma Bautista,
your creative talents live on!

many thanks to...

F+W Publications
including Tricia Waddell, Tonia Davenport,
Marissa Bowers and Megan Lane Patrick

The Bautista family

The Elarmo family

Jason Alfonso

Autumn Durald

Maristelle Bagis

Melissa and Sarah Aquino

Christina Ferreira

Tony Lafon

Mikey Hajek   Aunti Pegi

Aunti Wendy and Uncle Jeff   Cindy O'Leary

Monica Martinek

Phyllis Nelson

Michael Vincent Photography
www.michaelvincent.com

PAINTING PAPER and FABRIC

Painting, to me, is playtime—no worries, no boundaries—exploration of color, texture and line.

I pop in a CD, blast the beats and float away into a magical playland. My approach to painting is very free and uninhibited. Much like when I was young, I have never lost that childlike spirit when I am creating art. With the exercises and examples in this book, I encourage you to work intuitively, randomly and quickly, and never wonder what to do next. Try everything. Pick out a color, drizzle paint, then drizzle the next and start scraping colors across the canvas, staining the papers with dripping dyes and letting the colors run to create vibrant backgrounds full of emotion, texture and color. Anything goes. Try mixing mediums—various paints, dyes, sumi inks, glitter-metallic crayons—and use various found tools and brushes to make striking, colorful works of art.

Because painting involves a bit of setup, whenever possible, I recommend spending a full day just painting, to create a stash of beautiful backgrounds. The following techniques explore painting on fabric and paper and are perfect for journals, collages and wall hangings. A few of my favorite techniques are stepped out, and I have provided swatches and ideas for a variety of other painting techniques. Remember when you were a child, creating a piece of art? No fear, no intimidation—no boundaries. Go back to those days of creative exploration, and let your inner child free your art spirit and creative soul.

9

dyeing paper towels

Different papers take paints in the most beautiful and random ways, creating unlimited amounts of textured backgrounds. Experimenting with dyes is a great way to start the painting process. I paint on a variety of papers and fabrics; nothing is off-limits, including paper towels! Paper towels are easy to come by and surprisingly durable to work with, so they are a good paper to start with. Let's get our fingers dirty!

10

CREATIVE TOOLBOX

DISPOSABLE PLASTIC CUPS

ASSORTED WATER-BASED MEDIA: INTERFERENCE, METALLIC AND OTHER ASSORTED FLUID ACRYLICS, LIQUID WATERCOLOR PAINTS, STAMP PAD REINKERS, SUMI INK OR ACRYLIC CALLIGRAPHY INKS

GLITTER

CRAFT STICKS

TWO-PLY PAPER TOWELS

PIPETTE (OR EYE DROPPER)

FREEZER PAPER

SPRAY BOTTLE FILLED WITH WATER

BRAYER

PAINTING SMOCK (OPTIONAL)

fyi

Some things to keep in mind, when dyeing paper towels:

* All water-based media is intermixable.

* Dipping into all three primary colors (red, yellow and blue) will create a muddy brown.

* Metallic paint will settle on the bottom of the cups; stir occasionally.

* Dyed paper towels can be created by cleaning brushes, cups and tools with them—never waste!

* Waterproof or solvent-based inks can create a gum-like solution when mixed with water-based mediums—it's best to avoid them.

* Papers dyed with watercolors will bleed when collaged together.

* A monoprint of a dyed paper towel can be created by placing it between two pieces of white construction paper and rubbing gently. (See page 30.)

* The mixed dyes and paints should be the consistency of liquid watercolor or ink.

SET UP YOUR DYES

Using a separate cup for each color, mix your choice of water-based media with a bit of water. The amount of water added will cause colors to be more or less intense. To create a metallic dye, add a few drops of gold or silver fluid acrylic or iridescent acrylic ink. To add sparkle, drop a pinch of glitter into your dye mixture. Stir dye with a craft stick.

idea

While the paper towel is damp from the dye, you can gently pull the two layers apart, giving you two dyed towels! Adhere fusible interfacing to a single-ply dyed paper towel and sew it into your collages.

FOLD AND DIP METHOD

This method creates controlled patterns. Fold a paper towel, experimenting with different folds. Squares, rectangles, triangles and accordion pleats will all produce different and interesting patterns. Dip the folded paper towel into various mixed-dye colors. (I usually use two or three colors.)

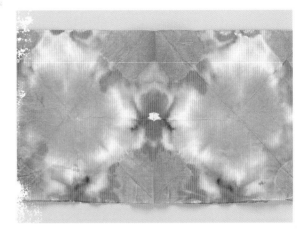

SCRUNCH AND DIP METHOD

This method creates free-form or tie-dyed patterns. Crumple a paper towel and dip it into various colors. Squeeze the paper towel to spread color. Take a pipette filled with a dye and squeeze onto the paper towel to spot dye and create lines of color. The colors will begin to run together in some spots, blending and creating new colors. (Take another paper towel, wrap it around the scrunched, wet one and squeeze out extra dye. You'll then have an extra dyed paper towel!)

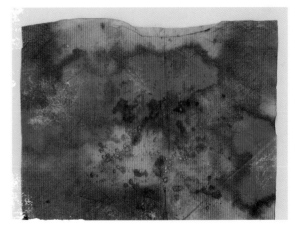

FREEZER PAPER DYEING

This creates random spotted patterns. Drizzle various watercolors, ink refills and fluid acrylics over the shiny side of a large piece of freezer paper. Sprinkle glitter and spray with a water bottle to disperse and mix colors. Place a paper towel down to pick up paint and continue to spray water to blend the colors on the paper towel. Repeat, adding color to the freezer paper. Brayer over the top until the paper towel is completely dyed. Drizzle interference colors over the top of the dyed paper towel.

color scraping

A simple color-scraping technique can give you an interesting texture over your painted background. After you have layered on paint, the color can be moved around with a paint scraper or other tools. I like to then accent over the top by stamping with heavy-bodied acrylics. Freestyle stitching (which we'll explore later) and accents of handwritten lettering with your favorite paint markers, gel pens, glitter writers and whiteout pens can finish off a color-scraped piece nicely.

12

MUSLIN, WATERCOLOR PAPER OR CARDSTOCK

VARIETY OF FLUID ACRYLIC PAINTS, OR HEAVY-BODIED ACRYLICS, THINNED WITH GLAZING MEDIUM PIPETTE, BRUSH OR CRAFT STICK

PAINT SCRAPER OR OTHER TOOLS TO SCRAPE WITH SCRAP PAPER OR CARDSTOCK

FOAM BRUSH

RUBBER STAMPS (HAND-CARVED OR COMMERCIAL)

FOAM SHAPES OR CHILDREN'S BLOCKS

GLITTER DIMENSIONAL GLUE
(SUCH AS STICKLES BY RANGER)

1. DRIZZLE PAINT

Randomly drizzle two or three fluid acrylic colors onto a piece of muslin or paper, using a craft stick, brush or pipette.

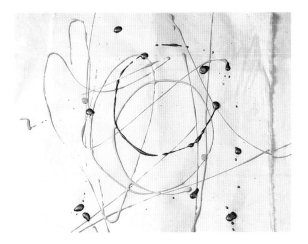

2. SCRAPE PAINT

Use a paint scraper to scrape across the fabric and move paint around; the colors will mix together to create beautiful new colors and patterns. Be careful to scrape each area only once. (Scraping over an area multiple times will continue to mix the paint, and sometimes will lose the pattern.) Place a second piece of cardstock or scrap paper next to the fabric to scrape the excess paint onto; this will also give you an additional piece of paper to use in your artwork later.

3. ADD A CONTRAST COLOR

Drizzle on another contrasting color and continue to scrape the paint around the fabric. Experiment with different scraping techniques; each will yield a different pattern. Continue to scrape until the entire piece of fabric or paper is covered with paint.

ideas

More options for adding texture and designs:
- ⚙ Use an adhesive spreader (or create your own out of cardboard) and use to comb through paint.
- ⚙ Create added glitz with glitter, beads or foil.
- ⚙ Use bubble wrap or sequin waste to add patterns.

4. STAMP DESIGN

Apply a contrasting paint color with a foam brush to an un-mounted stamp and press the stamp onto the painted fabric. Repeat stamping until you're satisfied with the pattern. If you're using heavy-bodied acrylics, add a bit of acrylic glazing medium to the paint so that you can work with it longer.

5. STAMP PATTERN

Add paint to another stamp in a different color and stamp a design.

I prefer to use unmounted stamps because I use acrylic paints to stamp with and, after using the stamps, I toss them into water so the paint doesn't dry on them. This practice might damage wooden mounts.

6. USE KIDS' TOOLS OR TOYS

Use kids' foam shapes to stamp over color scrapes for added contrast. It's good to have a variety of sizes with your stamps because it makes the composition more interesting. Here, I've used a small rectangle to make a border, a large flower and a medium square (which is actually a child's building block).

7. ADD SPARKLE

To finish off your piece, doodle or write with tubes of glitter dimensional paints (with fine tips) to accent some of the stamped designs.

crayon techniques

crayon cupcakes

Crayons. Broken crayons, metallic crayons, multicolor crayons . . . who knew that this kids' medium would be great to use for painted backgrounds? I create crayon cupcakes in order to have multicolored pieces to color with. This is a great way to use up all of those broken bits! In this section you'll discover various ways to use the crayons in your artwork.

VARIETY OF CRAYONS, INCLUDING METALLIC AND GLITTER

DISPOSABLE MUFFIN TIN

GLITTER OR MICA FLAKES

OVEN

15

1. FILL TIN

Remove the paper wrappers and break crayons into small pieces. Cut apart the section of the muffin tin. Fill the bottom of one section with a layer of crayons; use a variety of colors, including a few metallic and glitter crayon pieces.

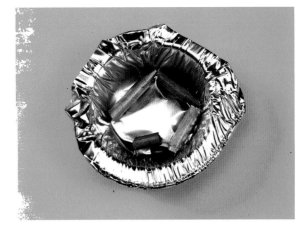

2. BAKE AND COOL

Sprinkle in glitter or mica flakes for added sparkle. Set the oven to 250° (121°C) and place the muffin tin in the oven until the crayons are melted (usually in 10–12 minutes). Turn off the oven and let the tin stand in the oven to cool. Do not move the muffin tin until the crayons have hardened, to prevent the melted crayons from over-mixing.

painting with crayons

Incorporating melted crayon into your work opens up a whole world of possibilities: melt them, smear them, mix them—create glorious metallic effects in your art. The waxy texture provided by crayons adds a uniquely new dimension.

CREATIVE TOOLBOX

- CRAYONS OR CRAYON CUPCAKES (SEE PAGE 15)
- TRAVEL IRON
- CARDSTOCK
- QUILTING IRON
- WOODEN SKEWERS
- DISPOSABLE MUFFIN TIN SECTION
- HEAT GUN
- NEEDLE-NOSE PLIERS
- TEXTURED WALLPAPER, STAMPS OR OTHER ITEMS FOR TEXTURE
- WOOD-BURNING TOOL, WITH CHISEL TIP

1. SMEAR CUPCAKE

Smear a crayon cupcake directly on a heated travel iron, then smear the melted wax onto the cardstock.

2. ADD METALLIC CRAYONS

Continue applying wax until the paper is full of crayon, and then create texture by pressing with the iron and lifting straight up. Interesting highlights can be added with metallic crayons. Draw swirls onto your iron and print over the background.

3. SWITCH TO QUILTING IRON

Smear a crayon or crayon cupcake directly on a heated quilting iron, then smear the melted wax onto the cardstock.

4. MELT FOR DRIZZLE

Another way of using the wax is to break up a crayon into a section of a disposable muffin tin. Melt the pieces with a heat gun.

5. POUR

Hold onto the tin with a pair of pliers and drizzle the melted wax over the paper in random puddles.

17

6. ADD STAMPED TEXTURE

Use the heat gun to remelt the wax and blow it around to thin it out a bit. Hold the paper upright and let the wax run down the paper. Rotate the paper in different directions for variety. While the wax is hot, stamp into it with a stamp or an item with texture, such as a piece of textured wallpaper. When heating the wax, be careful not to melt any area that you've already stamped.

idea

You can heat the paper with the iron and then draw with the crayon on the paper, for variety. I like to draw swirls onto the hot paper. Be careful not to heat the paper for too long, or you will burn it.

7. DOODLE

Use a wood-burning tool to doodle into the wax in some of the areas where the crayon is excessive.

8. ACCENTUATE YOUR DOODLES

Highlight areas of the wax where you doodled with a creamy crayon.

before we move on

We can't go on to the next chapter before I share a few last tips with you on using crayons, adding texture, using alternative tools, and uses for your painted papers.

ALTERNATIVE TOOLS FOR PAINTING

Why stick to only brushes for painting? Try using some of these alternates, instead!

foil
sponges
foam
blocks
foam brayers
alphabet
blocks
alphabet
rubber stamps
paint
scrapers

masking
tape ball
toothbrushes
pipettes
plastic utensils
craft sticks
straws
credit cards
with cutout
notches
cardboard

skewers
foam plates

chunky,
deeply-etched
rubber stamps

string

expandable
sponges

wax paper
freezer paper

QUICK IDEAS FOR USING CRAYONS

Now that you know how fun it is to use crayons in your artwork, here are other ways to consider using them.

* Try pressing different things into the melted crayons to get different effects. (See Texture Toolbox, below.) Be careful, as your fingers can get burned easily.

* Try different colors of paper.

* Add an ink or watercolor wash over the dried crayon, which will act as a resist.

* Draw onto the hot iron with a metallic crayon (with its paper peeled off). Press the design into paper. This works great as a contrast over other melted colors.

* When you want to change the colors that are melted on your iron, just wipe the iron off while it is warm and add new crayon pieces. I prefer the small chunks to shavings so the colors don't over-blend.

* Sprinkle glitter in the hot crayon that is on the paper.

* Use a small travel iron (without holes) to move the melted crayon around the paper. Use a small quilting iron for fine details.

* Alternative Technique: You can also use a hot plate from the thrift store, in lieu of an iron. Use something heat-safe, such as a craft stick, to swirl the colors together on the plate as desired, or make patterns, then lay a piece of paper down on the hot plate to print from it.

FANTASTIC IDEAS FOR PAINTED PAPERS AND FABRICS

When you start to think about all of the ways you can apply your painted background papers to other applications, you'll want to begin creating stacks right away. Here are some of my favorite ways to use up these papers:

Use painted pieces as they are for things like:

Base for collage

Covers of books, endpapers

Base for scrapbook title tiles

Signature covers in handmade books

Foundation for artist trading cards

Hanging ornaments and cones

Origami

Envelopes

Name cards

Color swatches

Or, take things a bit further and spruce-up your painted creations by doing the following:

Use as scrapbook paper

Die-cut machine tags and other shapes out of them

Apply image transfers over them

Manipulate scans of them in Adobe Photoshop

Add hand-stitched embroidery

Stamp images on them

Cut them up and use as "mosaic tiles"

Cut paper art-doll dresses out of them

Use them as quilling strips

Doodle with glitter pens on them

Layer transparencies over them

Use rub-on letters over them

Stencil onto them

Use them as scraps in an art quilt

Make rollup beads from them

SURFACE DESIGNS ON FABRIC

There are so many possible ways to use paint on fabric. Here is a quick reference you can use for instant inspiration when you need a little jump start to get you going!

1 Color scrapes on pre-quilted muslin. 2 Doodle scratches in paint on cotton fabric. 3 Bubble wrap patterns over color-washed fabric, accented with doodles from white dimensional paint. 4 Paint applied to an unmounted stamp and pressed onto fabric, then drizzled with red and purple paint, color-scraped and stamped with a square foam tool. 5 Color-scraped fabric accented with a free-form stitched floral shape. 6 Blocks of color created with masked-off sections from tape, then accented with different block patterns painted with a flat brush, and doodle lines added with metallic gel pens. 7 Words printed onto prepainted inkjet fabric. 8 Glitter sprinkled over wet, stamped squares. 9 Glitter markers and crayons written over color-washed muslin.

1 White acrylic paint applied to bubble wrap and stamped over a purple wash. 2 White space remaining on color-scraped fabric given a bright green wash. 3 Turquoise paint applied to an unmounted stamp and pressed onto muslin. 4 Print on fabric made by rolling out paint and glaze onto acrylic sheet with a brayer, then doodling into the paint with the end of a brush. 5 Girlie glam image scanned into computer and printed on inkjet fabric sheets. 6 Turquoise, pink and purple paint scrape. 7 White-on-white quilting fabric dip-dyed in blue and purple acrylic paint washes. 8 Red and lime stamped canvas. 9 Words written on canvas with a permanent marker. 10 Turquoise blue wash over red stamp print. 11 Blue and purple dip-dyed muslin. 12 Sumi ink eyedropper doodles over color-washed cotton fabric. 13 Glitter paint accents over stamped red square. 14 Dimensional paint doodles, washed with pink and purple.

SURFACE DESIGNS ON PAPER

These are not only great to try on paper, make sure to try some of these techniques on a variety of fabrics, too!

1 Newsprint scrunch-dyed with liquid watercolors. 2 Freezer paper print, with stamped texture. 3 Paint scraped onto a piece of cardstock, (glass shards dropped into paint for sparkle). 4 Texture on cardstock with spackle, then washed with watered-down acrylic paints, using a flat brush. 5 Random paint scrapes. 6 Crayon melt spread with a quilting iron using three crayon colors. 7 Crayon melt applied over tissue layered with gel medium. Text was burnished over the medium with a bone folder, for a transfer. 8 Paint applied to textured wallpaper, then pressed onto color-scraped cardstock. 9 Alcohol-based inks drizzled onto glossy paper spread around to create a marbled pattern. 10 Ink brushed randomly onto newsprint and then when dry, crumpled, dip-dyed and left flat to dry again. 11 Glass bead gel medium mixed with metallic bronze acrylic paint, spread onto cardstock, and scratched randomly with a skewer. 12 Color-scraped deli paper accented with stamped acrylic painted patterns. 13 Paper towel, wet with dye, placed between two pieces of drawing paper, and burnished with a brayer. 14 Acrylic paint mixed with spackle and painted through a stencil. 15 Dimensional paint accents over painted textured cardstock. 16 Painted background, printed with stencils that were brushed with paint, then pressed on the paper. 17 Print made by turning a freezer paper printing plate that has a design scraped into the paint, onto a piece of painted paper. 18 Washed paint over tissue paper, layered with gel medium and accented with drips of gold melted crayon. 19 Crumpled black construction paper, with brushed-on metallic copper paint. 20 Fluid acrylic paint, drizzled onto freezer paper, with sprinked metallic powder and glitter. (Repeated several times.)

TECH—TALK: COLOR THEORY

Being familiar with the color wheel not only helps you mix colors when painting but also can aid you in adding color to all your art creations. If you prefer a softer look to your artwork, try limiting your palette to three colors that are next to each other on the wheel, such as violet, red-violet and red. But, if you really want your colors to sing out loudly, work in hues that are opposite one another on the wheel, like blue and orange.

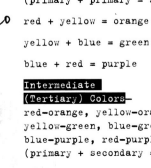

red-violet

red-orange

violet

red

orange

blue-violet

blue

orange-yellow

yellow

blue-green

green

yellow-green

Here are a few more color terms for you to know:

COLOR VALUES—the lights and darks of a color

TINT—a lightened value of a color; white + color

SHADE—a darkened value of a color; color + black

Primary Colors—red, yellow, blue
(no colors can be mixed to make these, but with them on hand, you can make any color that you like)

Secondary Colors—orange, green, purple
(primary + primary = secondary)

red + yellow = orange

yellow + blue = green

blue + red = purple

Intermediate (Tertiary) Colors—
red-orange, yellow-orange, yellow-green, blue-green, blue-purple, red-purple
(primary + secondary = intermediate)

Layers of color

PRINTING, STAMPING and USING *transparencies*

Combining colorful layers of images and textures can create a real richness in your artwork.

In this chapter, we'll explore a variety of simple printing methods created by painting directly onto the printing plate and then burnishing by hand. That is, printing without a press. I like to incorporate my own hand-carved stamps and handmade stencils with my printing plates, which are made of cardboard and foam. I'll show you fun methods, such as the monoprint sandwich and doodled monoprints. This chapter will expose you to different ideas for adding your own mark with printmaking.

My introduction to transparent art happened a little over ten years ago when I was in college. I created "overlays" to spec out type and layer images over painted backgrounds for my graphic design projects. In design production, these were pieces of acetate printed with typography, rub-on letters and laser copies of my original illustrations. I have taken this art technique a step further to create an endless amount of transparent pieces to incorporate into my artwork. The possibilities are endless. You can create your own transparencies and alter them, layer them, use different attachment techniques and create entirely new art pieces with the photocopy machine. Transparencies can be incorporated into various art projects, including artist trading cards, business cards, invitations, book covers, envelopes and wall hangings, or as accents to fabric journals and tags.

25

creating printing plates

26

Making a print is as easy as transferring paint or ink from one surface onto another. With a few simple found tools and objects, you can achieve your own unique prints that are always one-of-a-kind. Creating your own printing plates is fun, inexpensive and easy! Shown on the following pages are seven creative and super-simple ways to make a print.

CREATIVE TOOLBOX

HEAVY-BODIED ACRYLIC PAINTS

ACRYLIC GLAZING MEDIUM

BRAYER

ACRYLIC SHEET OR FREEZER PAPER

CARDSTOCK

CRAFT KNIFE

CRAFT GLUE

ASSORTED SCRAPS OF TEXTURED PAPER AND FABRIC

CARDBOARD

CIRCULAR ITEMS SUCH AS CUPS, PLATES OR BUBBLE WRAP

SELF-ADHESIVE FUN FOAM

FOAM GARDEN KNEELING PAD

WOOD-BURNING TOOL

ACRYLIC SHEET
OR FREEZER PAPER

Using a brayer, roll out paint and acrylic glazing medium onto an acrylic sheet or a piece of freezer paper. Doodle onto the wet paint with dimensional paints or reinkers, then make a print by laying down a piece of cardstock or paper over the sheet and burnishing with your hand. (Burnish lightly, if you're using a lot of paint.)

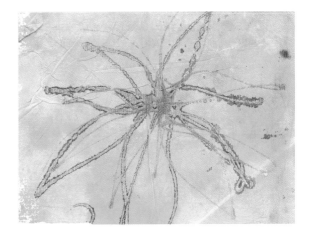

CUTOUTS AND
HAND-CUT STENCILS

Use a craft knife to cut a design out of cardstock. Now you have both a positive and negative stencil to use in your printmaking. (See Stencils and Textured Wallpaper, page 29.)

TEXTURED PLATES

Create a textured printing plate by gluing various pieces of handmade and textured papers and cloths to a piece of cardboard. I like to use lace paper, corrugated cardboard, cheesecloth and textured wallpaper.

FUN FOAM PLATES

This is created with self-adhesive fun foam. Cut shapes out of the foam and peel off the adhesive. Stick the shapes onto a piece of cardboard to make a printing plate.

To create circular designs in my artwork, I use a variety of tools such as the bottoms and tops of plastic cups, the edges of foam rollers and bubble wrap. To try this yourself, dip the end of the circular item into paint and use it to stamp the design.

CARDBOARD CUTOUTS

Cut random shapes out of cardboard and glue them to another piece of cardboard, using craft glue. Use these cutouts as you would use stamps, to print with.

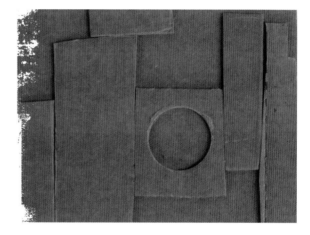

HANDMADE DOODLED STAMPS

I walked into a store and saw these bright garden kneeling pads and said, "These would make great stamps!" I cut the pads into small squares and rectangles and used a wood-burning tool to doodle onto the surface. The tool melts the design into the pad, and I use the top and bottom to get two stamps in one!

layering prints

Creating beautiful backgrounds,
by using a series of painting and
layering techniques, is fun and
easy! This unique method combines
the immediacy of painting with
printmaking methods. Learn about
glazing, washing and overprinting
designs with stamps and stencils to
create beautiful papers to use in
a variety of projects.

monoprint sandwiches

By taking a monoprint of your dyed
paper towels you can produce a lot
of glorious papers in a short amount
of time, and you won't waste any
paint! By sandwiching in texture
tools like stamps, stencils and
textured wallpaper you can yield
amazing results.

CREATIVE TOOLBOX

DISPOSABLE PLASTIC CUPS

ASSORTED WATER-BASED MEDIA: INTERFERENCE,
METALLIC AND OTHER ASSORTED FLUID ACRYLICS;
LIQUID WATERCOLOR PAINTS; STAMP PAD RE-
INKERS, SUMI INK, OR ACRYLIC CALLIGRAPHY INKS

TWO-PLY PAPER TOWEL(S)

PIPETTE

CARDSTOCK

STENCILS
(SEE CUTOUTS AND HAND-CUT STENCILS, PAGE 27)

TEXTURED WALLPAPER

BRAYER

STENCILS AND TEXTURED WALLPAPER

1. SET UP DYES

Prepare at least five cups with different colors and mediums,
all diluted to a liquid watercolor consistency.

2. DIP INTO DYE

Dye a paper towel by dipping different sections of it into
the different dyes, while it's wadded up. (You can use a
pipette to fill in certain areas for details of color.)

3. SET UP LAYERS

Set the unfolded paper towel (still wet with dye) on top of one piece of cardstock. Lay various stencils (paper or any other type) on top of the paper towel.

4. ROLL AND PRINT

Set a piece of textured wallpaper over the stencils on the paper towel, with the texture side down. Roll over it with a brayer. Lift and repeat over several sections. Lift off the wallpaper, stencils and paper towel to reveal the monoprint.

STENCILS AND FOLDING

1. CREATE FOLDS

Set the dyed paper towel (still wet) on a new piece of cardstock, but lay it down with some folds to it. Set a stencil (or two) on top of the paper towel.

2. ROLL RANDOMLY

Set a second piece of cardstock on top of the towel and stencil, then randomly roll over the paper with the brayer. Separate the papers from the towel and stencil and you are left with two prints, a positive and a negative.

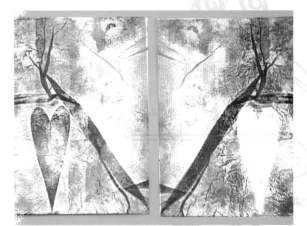

stamps and heavy-bodied acrylics

Acrylic paint and your commercial or hand-carved stamps offer a very graphic way to create layers and visual texture.

DYED PAPER TOWEL

CARDSTOCK

UNMOUNTED RUBBER STAMPS

BRAYER

ACRYLIC GLAZING MEDIUM

HEAVY-BODIED ACRYLICS

FOAM BRUSH

Using a glaze is a great way to tie together dyed or color-scraped backgrounds. To apply a glaze, dip your brush into water, then into a mixture of acrylic paint and acrylic glazing medium. The glazing medium allows you to work with the paint longer and creates layers that are slightly translucent. Brush over the surface of your paper, which will fill in the white space on your paper and unify the background. Use a clean paper towel to wipe back the glazed surface after paint is applied. The glazing medium changes the paint color slightly. Experiment with different colors.

31

1. RELIEF-PRINT WITH STAMPS

Set the dyed paper towel on a new piece of cardstock. Set a rubber stamp facedown on the paper towel and roll over it with a brayer. Repeat in different sections. Remove the paper towel to reveal the print.

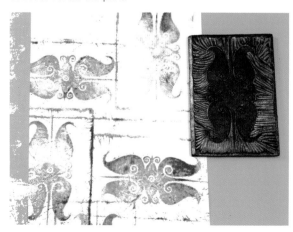

2. WASH OVER THE PRINT

Mix one part acrylic glazing medium to one part of the heavy-bodied acrylic color of your choice, and wash over the monoprint paper, using the brush of your choice.

3. ADD PAINT TO STAMP

Mix one part acrylic glazing medium to one part of a
different heavy-bodied acrylic and, using a foam brush,
apply it to a stamp. Stamp onto the paper, repeating the
image a few times.

4. REPEAT WITH SMALLER STAMPS

Mix up a third and fourth color with more glaze, and
stamp with two new stamps onto the paper.

5. CONTINUE OVERSTAMPING

Apply the acrylic paint in a different color to an unmounted
stamp with a foam brush. Press the stamp onto the painted
paper. Repeat stamp designs with various glazed colors
to create patterns over the top of the painted background.

doodle monoprints

Here's a fast and fun way to add a simple image to your artwork by drawing into the paint and making a print. Depending on the amount of paint that you use, you can sometimes get more than one print from the same plate.

CREATIVE TOOLBOX

PREVIOUSLY CREATED MONOPRINT
(SEE STENCILS AND FOLDING, PAGE 30)

ACRYLIC PAINTS

ACRYLIC GLAZING MEDIUM

PAPER TOWEL(S)

HEAVY-BODIED ACRYLIC PAINTS

ACRYLIC SHEET OR FREEZER PAPER

FOAM BRUSH

SKEWER OR OTHER POINTY TOOL

DIMENSIONAL PAINT WITH A FINE TIP

TEXTURED WALLPAPER

STENCILS AND STENCIL CUTOUTS

BRAYER

33

1. LAY-DOWN COLOR

Mix glazing medium and the acrylic color of your choice and wash over the previously created monoprint. Rub off the excess paint with a paper towel. Set this print aside. Brush a mixture of a heavy-bodied acrylic color and glazing medium over a sheet of acrylic or a piece of freezer paper, using a foam brush.

2. SKETCH INTO PAINT

Now, sketch into the paint using any pointy tool, such as a bamboo pen, a skewer or a knitting needle. If you want to write text, you will need to write it backwards because we are going to use this as a plate to make a print. Add additional doodles with a tube of dimensional glitter paint.

3. BURNISH PRINT LIGHTLY

Place the acrylic sheet or freezer paper facedown on the washed monoprint and rub over the back with your fingers. The print shown here is subtle because I used light pressure.

4. PRINT WITH MORE PRESSURE

The amount of pressure you apply and the dampness level of the paint will have an effect on the finished product. Here, the paint was wetter and I pressed harder; you can see the effect is very different from the previous image.

5. STAMP WITH TEXTURED PAPER

Brush some paint onto a piece of textured wallpaper, using a foam brush, and stamp with it onto the monoprint.

6. ADD STENCILED IMAGES

Try using a stencil. Set anything that could act as a stencil, like a hand-cut stencil or sequin waste ribbon, over the monoprint and dab the paint on with a foam brush. Work from the edges of the stencil inward to avoid pushing paint under the stencil.

 Sequin waste is the strip of plastic that is left over from where sequins were punched out. Since it has become popular with crafters, you can now buy sequin waste at craft and rubber stamp stores.

7. STAMP WITH STENCIL CUTOUTS

Here, I printed with what was the cutout of the last stencil. (I cut out additional details, first.) Dab paint onto the cutout, then place it facedown on the print and cover it with a scrap of paper. Roll over the cutout with a brayer.

creating transparency-ready imagery

To create transparencies for my artwork, I start with black-and-white line art created from my original drawings, writings, doodles or computer-generated images. It is important to me to include my own marks in any piece I design, so if I'm going to use a commercial image, I will combine it with my original illustrations.

Once you have a piece of art that you are satisfied with, the next step is to print it on a transparency. The printing method you choose will determine the type of transparency to use. Transparencies are made for either laser or inkjet printers and copiers and can be found at office supply stores. I prefer to use transparencies for copy machines because it's faster.

CREATIVE TOOLBOX

ORIGINAL ARTWORK

TRANSPARENCY SHEETS APPROPRIATE FOR YOUR PRINTER OR COPIER

ideas for black-and-white line art

The transparencies that I make have little or no gray value or color and are strictly in black and white. To get this dramatic effect, the art that you plan on copying to a transparent sheet will either be reduced to high contrast black and white, or you can create line art at the get-go. Listed here are some of my favorite methods:

- Scan original drawings, photographs and doodles that are in your journals
- Layer text and letterforms in a graphics program such as Adobe Photoshop to create interesting backgrounds and patterns
- Type out words related to your project in Microsoft Word or in a similar word processing program
- Create handwritten words with a calligraphy pen
- Enlarge or reduce portions of journal pages and writing on a copier
- Stamp an image with permanent ink such as StazOn
- Adhere rub-on letters to a piece of acetate or paper
- Doodle or draw on paper with a permanent pen
- Layer transparencies on top of each other and make a photocopy
- Create a digital image with your business contact information for artist trading cards
- Transform color images and photos into black-and-white art using Adobe Photoshop or a similar program

altering transparencies

Now that you have created your own transparencies, you can use a variety of media to alter the color of your transparencies. Sometimes I like to jazz up the transparency, altering the design by painting the back with various acrylic paints or using gel pens to color the designs.

CREATIVE TOOLBOX

TRANSPARENCIES PREPARED WITH IMAGES

ACRYLIC PAINTS

FOAM BRUSH

GEL PENS

GLITTER

TEXTURE-MAKING TOOLS

PERMANENT MARKERS

HEAT-TRANSFER FOIL AND HEAT TOOL

37

PAINT DIRECTLY ON TRANSPARENCY

On the back of the transparency, brush on different colors of acrylic paint, sprinkle glitter, comb through the paint or stamp a pattern. You might also like to accent the top of the transparencies with glitter paint pens, gel pens or permanent markers. To create metallic effects, I use a heat-transfer foil, and iron over the top of the areas that have toner.

stitching and attaching transparent layers

There are many ways to layer transparencies in with your art. One of my favorite attachment techniques is stitching. I machine sew over hand-painted fabric and paper, and yes, even dyed paper towels, backed with interfacing. But there are a variety of techniques to attach transparencies such as handstitching with embroidery floss, riveting with eyelets, stapling or wrapping the corners with foil tape or colored tape.

CREATIVE TOOLBOX

TRANSPARENCIES PREPARED WITH IMAGES

ARTWORK TO LAYER TRANSPARENCIES ONTO SEWING MACHINE

EMBROIDERY FLOSS AND SEWING NEEDLE

RIVETS OR EYELETS AND SETTING TOOLS

STAPLER

ASSORTED COLOR TAPES

EXPERIMENT WITH DIFFERENT STITCHING

Begin with a painted piece of fabric, or a collage layered with paper and imagery. Use a sewing machine to stitch down some of your transparency images, then attach additional transparencies by hand with a needle and embroidery floss.

before we move on

I know you can't wait to learn what's next. Before we leave this chapter, however, I wanted to plant some seeds for other ways to add layers to your painted papers.

ADDITIONAL TRANSPARENCY APPLICATIONS

Transparencies are just so much fun to use. If you've not worked with them before, here are some of the great ways you might consider taking them a step further:

* Transparency Sandwiches: Who doesn't love a good sandwich? I attach two transparencies together with a piece of artwork between them. "Artwork" could be a dried flower, glitter, sequins, confetti, small fabric bits . . . anything that fits!

* Create metal tags with tin, fabric and a word transparency.

* Print an image onto one transparency, then print words in another color on a different transparency, and layer them together.

* Create a transparency sandwich, attach with eyelets, and wire-wrap the edges with beads and charms.

* Layer a transparency over a painted background, strips of painted paper or colored laser print and then make a photocopy. Use the photocopy as a layer in future pieces of art.

* Staple a transparency over an image and mesh.

The use of transparencies doesn't need to be limited to layered collage work. Here are some other things you can do with them:

* Make a transparency quilt by stitching the edges to pieces of hand-painted fabric and paper.

* Make a wall hanging of transparency sandwiches attached with eyelets, wire and beads.

* Cut out a square in the middle of a piece of painted illustration board and suspend a transparency sandwich with an image in the middle of the cutout.

* Make envelopes with see-through panels by layering a printed transparency onto a piece of cardstock or vellum and stitching the edges closed.

39

TEXTURE TOOLBOX

Wax and paint can both be manipulated with an assortment of tools and objects, most of which you probably already have floating around your house. Found-item textures are a great way to accent your painted papers. I collect found objects with interesting textures and keep a texture box. When I paint, I can pull out these fun tools to create fabulous textures in my paintings. Here's a list of what I have inside my box:

40

textured wallpaper

burlap

garden kneeling pad stamps
(see handmade doodled stamps, page 28)

cardboard textured
printing plates
(see page 27)

doilies

assorted sponges

cheesecloth

chopsticks

Popsicle sticks

lace

sequin waste

ribbon

rug hook canvas

dried leaves

hand-cut stencils
(see page 27)

bubble wrap

plastic and wire mesh

bottle caps

wine bottle corks

cardboard coffee cup cuffs

large background rubber stamps

yarns and string

netting

contact paper

carpet tape

nonskid shelf liner

old keys

sandpaper

rubberband ball

scrunched tin foil

plastic wrap

wire designs

costume jewelry

drywall joint tape

CREATIVE WAYS WITH PRINTMAKING

Now that you are really getting your feet wet (or at least your hands),
let me share with you some of the ways that I've experimented with printing.

Print from a cardboard plate

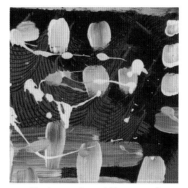

Print from a kid's foam block

Marks made with a comb
and drips of paint

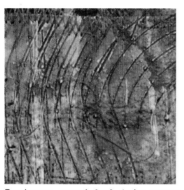

Print from bubble wrap
and hand-carved stamps

Textures scratched into gesso

Apply sticker dots
for a resist

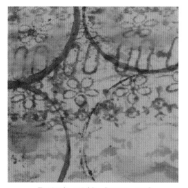

Print with lace and
drinking glasses

Paint through a stencil

Spray watercolor
through stencil

REVAMPING YOUR ART!

It's very important to leverage your artwork. I take my paintings and collage work and create black-and-white and color lasers of them to incorporate again and again into my other artwork. My journals are made up of a mixture of painted, stained and dyed papers, interlaced with copies of my artwork, color lasers and found papers. By finding ways to use your artwork over and over again, you create an endless supply of images to use in collage work and handmade journals. Here are a few ideas:

✱ Take digital photos or make scans at different stages during the process of making your art.

✱ Edit the digital images in Photoshop; play with the contrast and color levels.

✱ Take your printed photos or inkjet prints (or original versions) of your work to your local copy center and experiment with both the color and black-and-white copy machines. Also experient with size and with flipping or mirroring images.

✱ Send your doodles to a company that makes rubber stamps and have stamps made of your art that you can use over an over.

✱ Have your artwork printed on a postage stamp with the help of a company on the Internet such as www.photo.stamp.com or create your own faux-post using a store-bought rubber stamp template.

42

PHOTOCOPY MAGIC

Why do I love photocopies so much? Because it's a great way to leverage my art. As you can tell, I'm a great fan of working with copies. I just have so many ideas for using and making photocopies and here are the juiciest.

✱ Experiment with black-and-white copies using the following settings on the copier:
> text (will result in dark line art)
> photo/text (will result in a mixture of gray-toned and black art)
> photo (results in a grayscale photograph)
> printed image (results similar to photo)

✱ Layer a transparency over black-and-white art and then copy.

✱ Layer a copy printed on vellum over black-and-white art—it results in a ghosted copy.

✱ Photocopy areas of a large painted canvas.
(You'll see things differently when they are isolated and removed from their original context.)

✱ Copy handwritten words onto a transparency, and then layer it over painted paper.

✱ Take a printed alphabet in your favorite font and enlarge to make interesting black-and-white art for collage. Layer a transparency copied with a dictionary page over the enlarged font copy and create another new piece of black-and-white art.

✱ Create brush marks with sumi ink and enlarge or reduce to create more black-and-white art for collage.

✱ Copy your images in the negative setting and all the black turns to white and white turns black.

✱ Copy art onto iron-on transfer paper and transfer image onto fabric with an iron. Color with fabric markers or gel pens.

✱ Make funky fashions out of color laser copies of painted backgrounds to dress up pictures of people or to create paper dolls.

✱ Copy onto hand-dyed paper towels: Split the layers of a dry paper towel into two single plies, then use temporary spray adhesive to adhere one ply to a piece of copy paper. Run the piece through the self-feed tray.

43

POETRY

Making your Mark

FREESTYLE LETTERING and *Doodling*

Doodling is something that I have done since I was young.

It's simple, random, fun and doesn't take much thought. I just put a pen to paper and let the marks flow. Lots of tools can be used to write with: whiteout pens, Crayola Spider Writers (one of my favorites), Sharpies, crayons, color pencils, highlighters, Chinese painting brushes, glitter paints and acrylic paints with fine-tip applicators, glue pens, bleach pens and markers. I've also used tools such as eyedroppers with India ink, cut-up craft sticks, chopsticks and feathers—anything you can dip into ink—to make marks with. I collect a variety of black pens, kids' markers, glitter writers and gel pens to produce beautiful lines of text and marks in my artwork.

Just start to doodle and make marks—in your journal, on paper, on napkins, on fabric . . . anything you can write on. Continually ask yourself, "What if I tried this? I wonder if this would work?" Add a swirl to the end of your letter. Make an outline of a letter and color it in with more doodles. Write words, letters or phrases that are layered on top of each other to create interesting effects. Try writing words from off the top of your head. If you get stuck, find a font that you like and try to copy the strokes. This is a way to practice and make marks. You can always tear up your practice papers later to add into your collage. Don't be afraid! You can't make a mistake. Develop your own style. Don't worry if your letters don't look exactly like those in the calligraphy books. Many of those artists have been studying lettering for years. Just relax, have fun and play!

doodle warm-up

Doodling doesn't have to be limited to board meetings and phone calls. This exercise will instantly boost your creative metabolism and free up your spirit of play. Remember, there are no rules. You can even close your eyes, if you like.

46

CREATIVE TOOLBOX

LARGE SHEET OF DRAWING OR CRAFT PAPER

COLORED PENCILS

ASSORTMENT OF BLACK AND COLORED MARKERS

GEL PENS

WHITEOUT PEN

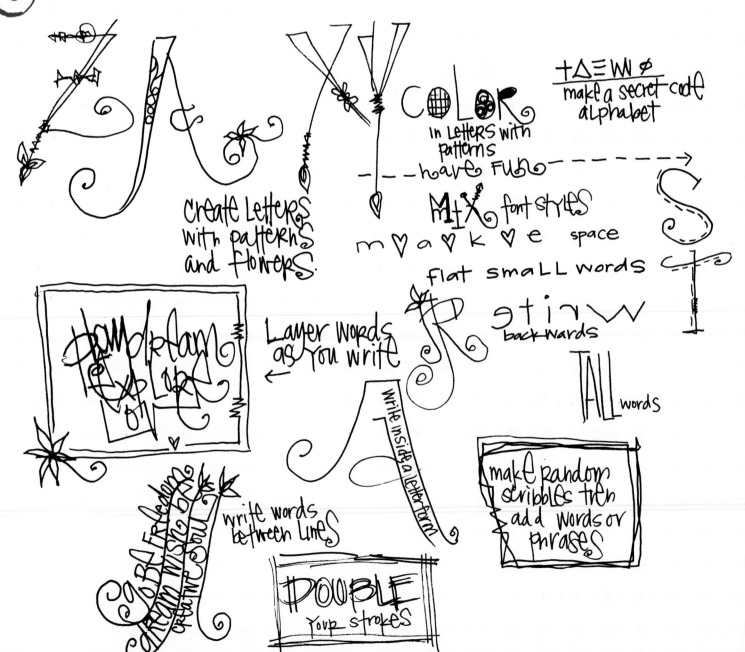

make a secret code alphabet

COLOR in letters with patterns

create letters with patterns and flowers.

have fun

MIX font styles

m a k e space

flat small words

write backwards

TALL words

Layer words as you write

write inside a letterform

write words between lines

make random scribbles then add words or phrases

DOUBLE your strokes

FILL A PAGE

Take a large sheet of drawing paper or craft paper and complete the following tasks: Write the alphabet (large), over the entire piece of paper, using colored pencils or markers. Next, write words that describe your day over the top of the alphabet. Continue to fill your paper with doodles and patterns, such as geometric shapes, floral patterns—whatever strikes you— using gel pens, markers and a whiteout pen, alternating colors. Experiment with writing letters short and tall, wide or with a swirl. Write randomly over the page. Don't think about placement, just work fast, and let the words and marks flow! Use the finished piece as it is, in collage work, or make copies of it to use in future projects.

ALPHABET EXEMPLAR I

This alphabet was written with a fine-tipped, oil-based gel pen. After creating the letterforms, I added accents of flowers and swirls.

ALPHABET EXEMPLAR II

By altering the way I use a calligraphy pen I can create my own funky alphabet.

48

girlie glam faces

One direction my doodles have taken is with the "girlie glam" art faces. My journals are filled with doodles of these girls; they're feminine, glamorous and pretty. I'll sit with my journal and a pen and let my strokes flow. Entwined with the girlie glam doodles are words and letters that have a relaxed but purposeful freedom to the forms. Layering doodles and text produces a variety of funky effects and depth in my artwork. The girlie glam doodles that have become a trademark of my art, are created with a fine-tip black pen.

CREATIVE TOOLBOX

FINE-TIPPED BLACK PEN

COLORED PENCILS

PIPETTE OR EYEDROPPER,
FILLED WITH INDIA INK (OPTIONAL)

ASSORTED PENS FOR COLORING (OPTIONAL)

49

FACES

My girlie glam faces are created at times when I'm sitting with my journal and just doodling. I don't start with any plan of what they will look like. Most of the time I use a black fine-tipped pen and start to draw the eyes with long, flowing strokes. Then, I continue to doodle the hair with long, swirly pen marks, adding in touches of flowers and leaves to the ends of the eyelashes and curls in the hair. Sometimes I will use an eyedropper filled with India ink to create the faces and then color them in with watercolor, colored pencils and various pens.

coloring doodles

Here's another creative way to leverage your art. Remember all those coloring books you used to color in when you were little? Well this is a take on creating your own grown-up coloring book. I like to take black-and-white photocopies of my doodles and drawings and change them by **adding** color. Learn how **to revamp** your art creations with a few tricks from colored pencils, markers, gel pens, glitter writers **and whiteout pens**.

50

CREATIVE TOOLBOX

PHOTOCOPY OF GIRLIE GLAM TEMPLATE (PAGE 123)

COLORED PENCILS

PORTFOLIO PASTELS

GLITTER WRITERS

CRAYOLA SPIDER WRITERS

GELLY ROLL GLAZE PENS

WHITEOUT PENS

GLITTER DIMENSIONAL PAINTS

1. MAKE COPY

Begin with a photocopy of the girlie glams from page 123.

idea

After coloring in your girlies like I have shown you here, you can use the finished piece whole, as a background, or cut up the images to use as embellishments in collage pieces.

2. COLOR WITH PENCILS

Color in the images with colored pencils. I like to begin by tracing over all of the lines with a variety of colors; then I might go back in and color in certain areas, such as the background. Don't assume you have to use realistic colors. In fact, it's more interesting if you don't.

3. PLAY WITH OTHER MARK-MAKERS

Other types of pens and mark-making tools can be used to further embellish your doodles. I have used pastels, glitter writers, Spider Writers, whiteout pens and gel pens. Remember, there are no rules; just use each as you are inspired to. Gelly Roll Glaze pens seem to work the best on top of colored pencil. The Spider Writers have more of a stringy effect, so I usually add details (such as highlights in the hair) with them last. The whiteout pens are used lastly, as well. Another media I like to use to further embellish are the glitter dimensional paints. Allow each of these mark-makers to dry between use to prevent smearing.

funky calligraphy

Break the rules! By altering the way I use a traditional calligraphy pen I have created my own funky lettering style. I love using sumi ink. It is traditionally used in Chinese brush painting, for lettering. I like the smooth opaque finish it has once it's dry. I dip my pen nib into the ink and, as I write letters, I use the broad tip to write the chunky parts. As I move to the end of a letter, I turn the pen to the side of the tip and use the point to create the thin serifs and swirly edges of the letters. Think beyond tradition and see if you can develop your own unique style.

ideas

Here are some quick ways for you to make funky letters:

- Dip nib into metallic pigments before writing.
- Write a wide alphabet with a chisel tip and color over the edges with paint markers.
- Write a scratchy alphabet.
- Find a few of your favorite fonts and try to combine pieces of each, together in one letter.
- Write your words with black ink and doodle designs over the top with fluorescent gel pens.
- Make letters with multiple strokes.
- Write words with a pipette filled with watercolor ink.

graffiti lettering

My graffiti-style is a combination of funky calligraphy with a "girlie-urban" twist. I have never been formally trained in calligraphy but have always loved to letter in my own way. When I was younger I would carry around a Speedball book and practice the letters, but I always gave them my own twist.

Inspiration for my lettering is influenced by letterforms from a variety of sources such as graffiti, art history pictograms, symbols, Maori tattoos, typography, the art of Erté and kids' writing. The key to developing your own freestyle lettering (and doodling) is to continually play and experiment. I keep various journals that house my scribbles, and whenever I have a chance, I take out my black pen and start to doodle.

WRITE WORDS IN LAYERS

Write words and phrases with a chisel-tipped marker, varying the size of letters. Write more words with various-sized markers including glitter or gel pens. Accent words with flower doodles and sketches. Continue to layer words and write out your sentences in varied sizes. Try writing with whiteout pens, over previously written words, to add contrast.

layering
freestyle lettering

By layering words, phrases and marks with various pens and different lettering styles, you can create even more depth to your lettering. I write large and work randomly across a canvas, moving it as I write—turning it upside down, writing in swirls, writing until the words look like a series of marks . . . sometimes illegible, but by layering letters and strokes you create interesting effects and backgrounds.

lettering on fabric
with iron-on transfers

Learn how to create graffiti lettering patches to incorporate into your fabric projects. By printing your work onto iron-on transfer paper, you can use imagery that you might not normally be able to get onto the fabric.

54

CREATIVE TOOLBOX

IRON-ON INKJET TRANSFER PAPER

INKJET PRINTER

ASSORTED MARKERS, COLORED PENCILS, GEL PENS

OIL-BASED BLACK GEL PEN

SCISSORS

COTTON FABRIC

IRON

PARCHMENT PAPER

FUSION-DYED COLLAGE OR HAND-PAINTED PAPER

basic transfer

Iron-on transfers that are made for your inkjet printer are easy to use and easy to find at any craft store. While I like printing out my transfers in black-and-white, you might like to experiment with printing in color.

Print out your art design on iron-on transfer paper. Cut out the design on transfer paper and iron it onto cotton fabric. The fabric here had a subtle white-on-white pattern that is still visible through the colored iron-on transfer.

transfer over gel pen

Because transfers are clear, you can layer them over writing or doodling that you've already layed down. Another option would be to iron the transfer over a fabric with a subtle pattern.

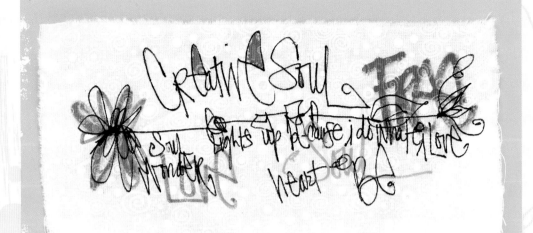

1. WRITE ON FABRIC

Write randomly on fabric with an oil-based gel pen, and color markers. Create doodles and also color in some of the letters.

2. PRINT OUT, IRON ON

Print out your design onto iron-on transfer paper. Cut sections of different designs that you can piece together for a mosaic look. Place a piece of parchment paper over the iron-on transfer and iron the individual designs onto a new piece of cotton fabric.

doodling directly on transfer

It's hard to stop with the doodling—so don't!
You can continue to make marks on top of the
transfers, even after they're ironed on.

DOODLE ONTO TRANSFER BEFORE IRONING

Draw, doodle and write directly on the iron-on transfer paper with various markers, pens and colored pencils. Notice how I wrote my words backward, so that they would read correctly when I transferred them.

DOODLE OVER TRANSFER AFTER IRONING

Cut out a portion of the design that you want to use and iron it onto fusion-dyed collage, fabric or hand-painted paper. (If you try ironing onto paper, be careful not to burn or melt the paper.) Here, I have applied the transfer to white-on-white cotton fabric, then I doodled over it with a pen.

before we move on

Are you having fun adding your own writing and doodles to your artwork?
Let me share a few more tidbits with you, before we leave this chapter.

HINTS FOR WRITING ON FABRIC

Most fabrics will take a variety of mark-making tools. Experiment with what you have, and keep these tips in mind as you play:

✱ Tighter-weave fabrics such as cotton sheeting and some muslin are a great writing surface. Opaque gel pens work well on this type of fabric.

✱ Not all pens work as well on fabric, but always try them out. I've found that tools, markers or pens with wide tips work better on canvas-type fabrics.

✱ When writing on fabric, sometimes you have to go over the stroke two or three times to get a darker line.

✱ Once you have painted fabric with acrylic, you can write over the dried paint with gel pens, oil pastels, glitter paint writers and Spider Writers.

✱ Most of my work is not intended to wash, so I don't worry about the type of ink or paint I use. But if you want to make wearable art, you need to use a fabric marker or pen created for that purpose.

✱ You have to write more slowly than you normally would when you use fabric as your base.

57

MORE ALTERNATIVE MARK-MAKING TOOLS

These are things you can use after dipping them in ink or paint:

craft sticks   eyeshadow applicators

natural sticks   cotton swabs

reeds/bamboo   chopsticks

toothpicks

coffee stir sticks

idea!

Freestyle lettering on fabric:
Make a pen sampler on fabric, using various pens, markers and pencils to create a sampler on a piece of white or black cotton. This will be a guide, so you can remember which pens work on cotton fabric best.

ALTERNATIVE MARK-MAKING TOOLS

If it can make a mark on your paper or fabric, use it—it's a mark-making tool!
Here you can see some of the many ways I make my mark.

Oil-based gel pen
on fabric

Eyedropper marks

Colored pencil and calligraphy

Black pen and sequin waste

Craft sticks and glitter paints

Wide-tipped markers

Whiteout markers

1. ERTE doodles → choose your favorite part of an ERTE illustration & start to doodle

2. open a book and jot down the first ten words you read. Copy a phrase. turn the page. Copy more words then write them backwards

3. Flip through a magazine, study the lines of a picture doodle those lines

4. Find a font you like and alter it with Random flower doodles

5. Look at things in nature. take a walk and pick up a leaf, flower, etc. and use it as the inspiration for your doodles.

6. Fast doodle starts...
   - make dots on your paper... Connect the dots... with wavy, scratchy or flowing lines
   - make random scribbles with your pencil
   - draw shapes and fill them in with patterns like lines, circles or hearts
   - draw repeating shapes
   - doodle swirls

Most of all Have fun. Be free. Make random marks → JUST PLAY

59

total fusion

COMBINING
collage styles

Accents of freestyle letters and words, hand-dyed paper—the paint drips and fall where it falls.

Photocopies of my original "girlie" sketches and doodles, a little tape, textured lace papers, staples, mark-making with fat-tipped black permanent markers, lines and swirls from brushes loaded with sumi ink . . . drips from spray paint, washes of bright, vibrant color that spills all over the canvas . . . . accents with acrylics, paint streakers, gel pens, glitter writers, paint markers and whiteout pens . . .

This is just a little insight into my world of collage—completely unleashed! Explore and experiment with a plethora of the mixed-media collage techniques that I will share with you in this section. Keep in mind that they can be used to create whatever size canvas you want, from small sizes that make great covers for journals to large wall murals. Explore. These are just the beginning basics, and you can take and twist them into your own art. Keep playing and exploring to create your very own masterpieces!

fusion-dyed collage

After teaching art workshops for children, I found **paper towels** to be an inexpensive alternative to high-end **rice paper** for the Japanese art of dyeing paper known as orizomegami. With stacks of dyed paper towels accumulating in my studio, **fusion-dyed collage** was born!

This technique merges layers of dyed paper towels, ephemera and paint to create beautiful transparent, textured pieces of art. They are great as they are, but I also incorporate the collages into journal covers, and, I sew them into wall hangings.

CREATIVE TOOLBOX

ELMER'S GLUE-ALL OR PVA

WATER

DISPOSABLE CUP

2-INCH (51MM) FLAT BRUSH

FREEZER PAPER

DYED PAPER TOWELS (SEE PAGE 10)

SCISSORS

DELI PAPER

PHOTOCOPY OF DOODLES OR ANY LINE ART
(IMAGES OR WORDS)

SOFT GEL GLOSS MEDIUM (GOLDEN)

SEWING MACHINE FOR
STITCH EMBELLISHING (OPTIONAL)

transparent technique

This technique works great as a jumping-off point for layered collage, or as an end product in itself. The finished, dried layers are peeled up off of the freezer paper, and you are left with a beautiful, transparent collage of dyed paper towels.

LAYER PAPER TOWELS WITH GLUE

Mix four parts of PVA or Elmer's with one part of water in a large plastic cup. With a 2-inch (51mm) flat brush, spread the glue mixture over the shiny surface of an 18" × 30" (46cm × 76cm) piece of freezer paper, working in sections. Pull apart layers of pre-dyed two-ply paper towels. Place a single layer of the dyed paper towel onto the glued surface. Coat the top of paper towel with a layer of the glue mixture. Continue to layer dyed paper towels, overlapping the edges to fill the entire piece of freezer paper, coating each layer of the collage with glue as you go. Cut shapes such as hearts or flowers from the dyed towels and adhere them with the glue mixture, building up the layers of the collage. Let the collage dry completely. Once dry, peel it carefully from the freezer paper and you have a beautiful, transparent collage.

62

layering over images

This is the technique I find myself using the most frequently.
I love the subtle effect the images take on when only slightly
visible beneath the dyed paper towels.

1. PULL TOWELS FROM STASH

Begin by gathering some dyed paper towels that you've
made previously, such as when you were cleaning up your
paints or from dip-dyeing.

2. LAY DOWN IMAGES

Mix four parts of glue with one part of water in a disposable cup. Set a piece of freezer paper on your work surface.
Place a piece of deli paper over the freezer paper. Cut apart
various pieces of black-and-white art from your photocopies.
Using the 2-inch (51mm) flat brush, apply a layer of the glue
mixture to the deli paper, working in small sections, and
adhere the pieces of photocopies in a collage fashion. Brush
additional glue mixture over the tops of the images.

3. LAYER WITH PAPER TOWELS

Pull apart layers of pre-dyed two-ply paper towels. Cut or
tear the paper towels into sections. Place a single layer of
the dyed paper towel onto the glued surface. If the paper
towels are dry, dampen the sections a bit with water, and
then adhere them over the photocopy collage. Brush the
glue mixture over the tops of the paper towels. I like to fold
up the sections of paper towels that hang over the edge of
the deli paper.

4. LAYER ON SHAPES

Continue covering the photocopy collage with paper towel sections until it is full. Cut out shapes from the paper towels to collage over the sections that are already down.

5. APPLY GEL MEDIUM

Apply a layer of gloss gel medium over the finished collage, if you desire a glossy finish.

6. ADD STITCHING

After the collage is dry, you can use a sewing machine to create freestyle stitching, accenting the fusion-dyed collage with a contrasting colored thread. This highlights shapes and edges. Experiment with sewing on transparencies (see page 38) and with sewing freestyle images such as flowers (see page 92).

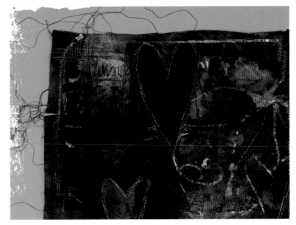

accenting over fusion-dyed collage

Here are a few ideas for building up designs over your fusion-dyed collages.

Apply heavy-bodied acrylics with a foam brush through stencils to create patterns.

Apply heavy-bodied acrylics with a foam brush to an unmounted stamp and stamp a pattern, then freeform stitch.

Paint repeating square patterns with flat brushes.

Write words and phrases over the top with Crayola Spider Writers, glitter paint writers or whiteout pens.

Paint ink drawings with a pipette using black sumi ink or waterproof india ink.

Drip melted metallic crayon over the top of the collage, then add acrylics.

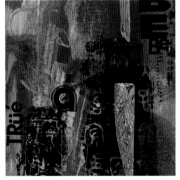

Use rub-on letters over the top of the collage.

Draw designs with water-soluble oil pastels and layer with painted cutouts.

Stitch on a photo and add freeform designs.

collage with words and symbols

I am fascinated with color, words and symbols from art history. I like to incorporate letters and symbols into much of my work by writing with a permanent marker, scribbling in gesso, or using photocopies of symbols and incorporating them into the first layer of my collage, even if the words are covered or are barely peeking through. I like to incorporate scans, pictures and copies of my journals, girlie faces and writings into my collage backgrounds, because it's a reminder of where my work has been and it's a tie to the past.

Make a collage that incorporates letters, words and symbols associated with the theme of your project. Using a textured layer of gesso, scratch designs into the base of your collage.

66

CREATIVE TOOLBOX

ROSIN PAPER

GESSO

FOAM BRUSH

MARK-MAKING TEXTURE TOOLS

GLAZING MEDIUM

HEAVY-BODIED ACRYLICS, INCLUDING SOME METALLICS

WATER-SOLUBLE PASTELS (PORTFOLIO)

ART STIX (PRISMACOLOR)

GEL PENS

HOT FOIL PEN (OPTIONAL)

GIRLIE GLAM IMAGE (OPTIONAL)

STAPLER (OPTIONAL)

 fyi

There are numerous places you can look to find symbols and inspiration:

✱ Art history
   (cultures, images and symbols from the past)

✱ Pictograms
   (symbols used to communicate ideas)

✱ Hieroglyphics
   (Aztec, Egyptian, Neolithic writings from China)

✱ Letters and letterforms
   (alphabet letters from all languages)

✱ Quilts (Adinkra cloth, medieval quilts, molas)

✱ Family crests (images and symbols representing family names)

✱ Patterns in nature (trees, leaves, petals, flowers)

✱ Fashion trends (magazines, fashion shows, music videos, movies)

✱ Master artists' techniques (Art Nouveau masters, Klimt, Beardsley and Erté are my favorite artists)

✱ Other artists' work (try to figure it out for yourself; you'll discover a bunch of new techniques)

✱ Travel to foreign countries

✱ Graffiti art and paintings

✱ Children's art (observe their freedom and playful art spirit)

1. DOODLE INTO GESSO

Cover a piece of rosin paper with gesso, using a foam brush. Create texture in the gesso with various mark-making tools. Set aside to dry.

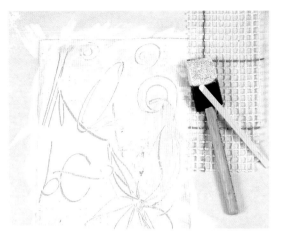

2. BEGIN ADDING COLOR

Wash over the gesso with a mixture of glaze and heavy-bodied acrylic. After the page is covered, load up the wet brush with lots of paint and press it on the top of the page. Hold the page up and let the paint drip down. Let the paint dry before moving on.

3. ADD COLOR STICKS

Apply color around the edge of the page with pastels, then use Art Stix to color over the gessoed areas and bring out the texture. I like to lay the sticks down flat and use the entire stick to rub on color. Use your finger to apply metallic paint to some of the raised areas.

4. WRITE WITH GEL PENS

Use gel pens to add lettering or any doodles that you'd like.

5. APPLY SILVER FOIL

Here, I have also added some doodling with a hot foil pen and silver foil. If you don't have one of these pens, you can use the tip of a quilting iron along with the hot foil, or you can use leafing adhesive and metallic leaf. Finish off your collage by stapling a girlie glam (or any other image) to the top.

textured paper collage

Create an interesting piece of art using handmade textured paper as the base of your collage. The beautiful, tactile texture of the handmade paper, combined with washes of color and stitching creates a vibrant result.

CREATIVE TOOLBOX

WATERCOLOR PAPER

PERMANENT MARKER

ASSORTED TEXTURED HANDMADE PAPERS

GEL MEDIUM

GLAZING MEDIUM

HEAVY-BODIED ACRYLIC PAINTS

FABRIC PAINTS (LUMIERE)

FLAT BRUSH

FOAM BRUSH

UNMOUNTED RUBBER STAMPS

SEWING MACHINE FOR STITCH-EMBELLISHING

1. WRITE OR DOODLE

Doodle or write words with the permanent marker to cover the watercolor paper.

2. LAYER ON HANDMADE PAPERS

Cut or tear apart various pieces of handmade papers and adhere them over the doodled paper with gel medium. Leave some of the doodled area to show through.

3. ADD HIGHLIGHTS

Wash over the papers with a mixture of glaze and heavy-bodied acrylics. Add metallic highlights with a Lumiere paint, using a flat brush. Set aside to dry.

4. STAMP IMAGES

Using a foam brush, apply paint or ink to the stamps of your choice and stamp onto the collage.

5. SEW ONTO THE FINISHED PIECE

Add stitching to create flowers or lettering.

washed photocopy collage

Black-and-white photocopies make a great background for collage. Paint, write and doodle over them! You don't need to limit yourself to copier paper, either. Many modern copiers will accept lighter-weight watercolor paper and most weights of cardstock.

70

CREATIVE TOOLBOX

PHOTOCOPIES OF BLACK-AND-WHITE LINE ART OR TEXT

CANVAS PAPER OR BOARD

SCISSORS

GEL MEDIUM

FLUID ACRYLICS, THINNED WITH WATER

2-INCH (51MM) FLAT BRUSH

PERMANENT MARKER

HEAVY-BODIED ACRYLICS

ORIGINAL PHOTO OR DRAWING

DECORATIVE BRADS

1. COVER CANVAS WITH COPIES

Using gel medium, glue several copies to a canvas. Wash over the papers with a mixture of glaze and heavy-bodied acrylics. Add metallic highlights with a Lumiere paint, using a flat brush. Set aside to dry.

2. APPLY WASH OF COLOR

Using watered-down acrylic paints, load a flat brush with two or three colors of paint and wash over the entire surface of the photocopy collage. Let dry.

3. WRITE WITH MARKER

Write over the top of the painted collage with a gel pen to add designs.

4. SCRATCH IN DOODLES

Paint a bright contrasting color of heavy-bodied acrylic paint mixed with a little gel medium to accent different areas of the collage. Scratch in doodles with the back of the paintbrush.

5. SECURE PHOTO

Adhere a photo or drawing over the top of the collage with rivets, brads or tape.

fabric-paper patchwork collage

My work incorporates both paper and fabric, and I treat each of them the same—I stitch, glue, sew, eyelet, pin, staple and tape, interchangeably. One of my favorite ways to combine these surfaces is with fabric and paper patchwork collages. I pull hand-painted scraps of each from my stash, and piece them together, using a sewing machine, randomly layering, with raw unfinished edges and strings hanging. As a finishing touch, I embellish them with transparencies and more free-form stitching, including funky flower designs and embroidery stitches. To create journal covers, I like to sew the quilts to silence cloth as a base. Used to make tablecloth covers, silence cloth can be found in the upholstery section of the fabric store. I usually sew with two different threads in the sewing machine: cotton thread in the bobbin and a different colored rayon thread for the needle. This creates pizzazz! Use quilts to embellish a T-shirt, to make a handbag, journal cover or as a wall hanging!

72

PAINTED SCRAPS OF FABRIC AND PAPER

UNPAINTED FABRIC SCRAPS

FUSION-DYED COLLAGE SCRAPS

GLUE AND PLASTIC SPREADER OR IRON-ON ADHESIVE (NO SEWING), PARCHMENT PAPER AND IRON

SEWING MACHINE

RAYON THREAD

SILENCE CLOTH

DYED PAPER TOWELS BACKED WITH IRON-ON INTERFACING

TRANSPARENCIES PREPARED WITH IMAGES

RIBBON SCRAPS (OPTIONAL)

1. GATHER FABRIC

Gather pieces of painted fabric and unpainted fabric scraps that accent one another.

2. PIECE FABRIC TOGETHER

Tear or cut pieces of fabric and begin joining them together. There are several ways to do this, my favorite being "sew as you go" where I attach one piece of fabric to another using a free-form zigzag stitch. I also like to stitch the pieces to silence cloth as a base. Instead of sewing, you can also "glue as you go" and appy glue to the back of the fabric as if it were paper, and collage it onto silence cloth. Finally, a third option is the "iron as you go" technique in which you can use an iron-on adhesive or webbing, and with a piece of parchment paper over your painted fabric pieces, iron the individual pieces to silence cloth or other backing fabric of your choice.

3. ADD FREE-FORM STITCHING

Now is the time to add free-form stitching like flowers or any other pattern you choose, using the reverse button to aid in your stitch "drawings."

4. ADD ACCENTS

To complete your quilt, try adding accents with pieces of fusion-dyed collage, transparencies, ribbons or couched fibers. (See page 77 for more on couched fibers.)

Sewn scraps attached to painted fabric with
free-form stitched flowers.

Painted papers stitched with handwritten
words and transparencies.

Transparencies stitched to fusion-dyed collage.

Painted fabric edges stitched
with free-form zigzag.

Dyed paper towels, scrunched and sewn to
interfacing, with free-form stitches.

Couched fibers and writing with gel pen.

Patchwork with couched fibers, brocade fabric and inkjet print of a girlie glam face.

Transparency sewn over dyed paper towels, attached to painted fabric and paper with free-form stitches.

Transparency layered over painted fabric and handmade paper.

Hand-painted fabric stitched together and layered with transparencies.

Color laser print, stitched to brocade and painted fabric.

tape collage

Tapes of all kinds and sizes work great in collage.
Tape is easy to find and any kind works! I've used duct
tape, masking tape, packing tape, electrical tape . . .
you name it. Here are some examples of my favorite ways
to work them in.

1 CLEAR TAPE

Cut painted papers, photocopies or color lasers of artwork. Adhere to a canvas
surface using clear packing tape, working on sections at a time until the entire
page is filled up with collage.

2 SPECIALTY TAPES

Accent with various colored tapes such as thin metal tape; label printed tape and strapping tape;
electrical tape and see-through fluorescent tape.

3 WORDS ON TAPE

Write words with permanent markers over the top of tapes or add words and symbols with rub-on letters.

collage flower

Create a funky floral collage embellishment by piecing together painted fabric, fusion-dyed collage and paper towels with freestyle machine stitching.

These freestyle flowers are my favorite image to "draw" with the sewing machine. But, while I like creating flowers, you might like to make houses or letters. The process for any freestyle stitching is the same.

CREATIVE TOOLBOX

DYED PAPER TOWELS

HEAVYWEIGHT INTERFACING

SEWING MACHINE

FABRIC SCRAPS AND PIECES OF FUSION-DYED COLLAGE

RAYON THREAD

SCISSORS

1. CRUMPLE AND SEW
Take a single ply of a dyed paper towel and sew it to heavyweight interfacing, scrunching the paper towel as you sew. Randomly sew stitches over the paper towel to create a background.

2. STITCH OVER COLLAGE
Add pieces of fabrics, fusion-dyed collage and more paper towels and continue to stitch randomly over the top with a contrasting rayon thread until the background interfacing is entirely covered.

3. OR, SEW ON STRIPS
VARIATION: Sew strips of various dyed paper and paper towels to the interfacing to create blocks of color.

4. CUT OUT FLOWER
Once you have created your textured piece, sew a free-form flower over the top, and cut out the design.

5. ATTACH FLOWER
Adhere the flower to a journal cover or to a handbag, with the method of your choice (glue or stitching).

fabric strip collage

Another way to add texture to your fusion-dyed collage or fabric-paper patchwork collage is with free-flowing lines that are created with thin strips of fabric. A free-form zigzag stitch secures the strips (this is known as "couching"), and sometimes it's fun to couch in decorative fibers or yarn. I prefer the thread color to contrast with that of the fabric and fibers, but you could coordinate them for just a small punch of color.

ASSORTED FABRICS

FABRIC SCISSORS

FUSIBLE INTERFACING

PARCHMENT PAPER

IRON

SEWING MACHINE THREADED WITH RAYON THREAD

ASSORTED FIBERS, YARNS OR RIBBONS

1. CUT OR TEAR STRIPS

Cut or tear fabric into strips that are 1/4" to 1/2" (6mm to 13mm) wide, by any length. I like to randomly cut strips with jagged, uneven edges. Mix and match colors, textures and patterns.

2. SECURE STRIPS WITH IRON

To keep the strips of fabric in place as you couch them onto the collage, back them with fusible interfacing first. Lay out the strips on the collage where you want them and place a piece of parchment paper over the collage. Iron the strips down, being careful with the heat, not to burn any painted fabric, or to remove any previously secured iron-on transfers.

3. COUCH ON FIBERS

Using a sewing machine and a zigzag stitch, randomly stitch over the top of the fabric strips. Couch on fibers or ribbons with contrasting threads.

4. ADD A FLOWER

Free-form stitch a flower over the top of the collage with a zigzag stitch. For fabric strip and fiber ideas, see Idea! on page 105.

before we move on

I bet you're looking at fabric with a new set of eyes now! The options of combining fabric, paint and paper for collage are endless, so here are some more ideas.

DECIDING ON A THEME

Sometimes deciding on a theme for a collage can be tough and prevent you from getting started. Consider these tips and sources:

✱ Start an idea book. Collect information—images, text, words, quotes, color swatches— and put them into an idea book. Add anything that is inspirational to you or related to a project you are working on. Staple, glue or tape it into your idea book.

✱ Create an Adjective Bank. Take two minutes to brainstorm ideas on a topic. Write down anything that comes to mind on a piece of paper. I like to brainstorm using a large piece of drawing paper taped to the wall.

✱ Look for ingredients and inspiration everywhere—always take notes.

✱ Scour media (magazines, movies, books).

✱ Look for ideas in art, fashion or music that you like.

✱ Enter a word or idea that you like in Google or other search engines, then see what comes up. This is virtual brainstorming!

DESIGN INSPIRATION FILE

When working on larger projects, create a design journal or file. Use the file or book in the following ways:

✱ Brainstorm in your journal.

✱ Paste samples into your journal.

✱ Put in your original sketches.

✱ Keep your journal close to you (in your bag, by your bed).

✱ Paste in computer developed concepts (keep notes).

✱ Date everything.

✱ Paste in Pantone chips, color swatches, fabric.

✱ Paste in images, magazine and newspaper clips or other things that inspire.

✱ Write down color schemes.

✱ Keep track of fonts.

✱ Keep track of search engine submissions.

✱ Keep track of final file names.

✱ Compile research in your journal.

✱ Glue or tape in a picture of the final project.

COLLAGE STARTERS

Stumped for collage starters? After washing a canvas or paper with color, jump right in and try one of these:

* Write big letters with tools on a light background.

* Create organic shapes and strokes; let your brush flow.

* Keep moving—don't slow your movement.

* Brush in a circular motion, creating a variety of swirls and circle shapes.

* Use a foam brush or Chinese brushes for washes.

* Wash on top of words.

* Write with a chisel-tip marker or Sharpie; use pictograms, hieroglyphics.

* Use oil pastels and create lines, then wash metallic acrylic inks between the lines.

* Use a credit card or paint scraper to scrape color onto your surface.

* If you make a wash you don't like, cut it up and collage it into another piece.

* Dip brush in walnut ink and then a metallic powder to create a wash.

* Write out text or a quote on a light background color with pen or fine-tip marker.

* Don't focus on the final product—let go . . . create . . . let your artwork flow.

idea!

Leverage your artwork by arranging multiple pieces of finished collages and patchwork quilts on a photocopier (to use in new artwork). It's collage on the photocopier!

wiLDly bound

STITCHING *bindings* *and* FUNKY *embellishments*

Wild and nontraditional are the words to describe the funky bindings I create in all of my books.

After you have spent some time exploring collage and painting papers and fabrics, you might begin to accumulate quite a stash, such as I have. So what can you do with your stash? I like to use simple techniques to create the illusion of wild intricacy. In this section we'll explore funky bindings such as free-form crochet, macramé with a twist, beaded wire and simple stitching. By altering the basics of these bindings you can create your own funky versions. I will take you through the basics of each binding style and offer creative variations to show how, with a little tweaking, you can create a completely new look.

What do you do with free-form stitching, wire and beads? Embellish, embellish, embellish. I like to finish off my art journals and fabric work with a variety of funky, free-form embellishing techniques. So, I'll also show you examples of different types of simple additions to your art journals, collages and art quilts. We'll finish things up with examples of some of my favorite embellishment ideas, such as stapling, embroidery and doodling in craft metal.

81

creating signatures

A book signature is simply a group of pages that have been folded and stitched together at the fold. Several signatures are then sewn together to form a book or journal. I prefer to use waxed linen thread for sewing papers together because it doesn't get tangled up very easily. It also holds its shape, so it doesn't loosen up over time.

CREATIVE TOOLBOX

FOUND PAPERS

PAINTED OR DYED PAPERS

CARDSTOCK

WHITE CRAFT GLUE

BONE FOLDER

SCRAP PAPER TO MAKE A TEMPLATE

RULER

PENCIL

BINDER CLIP

AWL

WAXED LINEN THREAD

PAPER SEWING NEEDLE

1. SELECT PAPERS

Using a mixture of found papers and painted or dyed papers, fold a small stack to make your first signature. Keep in mind that you are going to have to punch holes through all of the pages as they are stacked together, so work with an amount that is comfortable for you. Depending on the thickness of the paper, I usually use between six and twelve pages. They don't have to all be the same size. I prefer them to be various sizes, and I don't always fold them in half but sometimes off-center.

2. GLUE COVER TO CARDSTOCK

To make a cover for a signature (which is different from the cover for the entire journal), apply white glue to the center of a painted paper, scraping it all the way to the edges; then press the paper onto a piece of cardstock. Use a bone folder to rub the paper all the way to the edges. (You can see I was having a bit of fun with the glue here!)

3. FOLD THE COVER

After the glue dries, fold the piece of paper in half, matching up two corners. You can use a bone folder to score the center line to make the page fold better. Then use the bone folder to burnish the folded edge and make it lay flat.

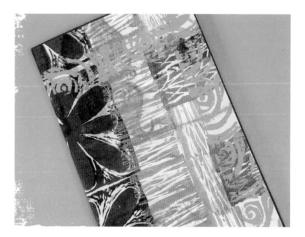

4. CREATE VARIETY OF SIZES

Place the folded papers from step 1 into the signature cover. Don't worry if the pages don't fit neatly between the covers. Let them spill out.

5. STACK FOLDED PAPERS TOGETHER

It's a good idea for the page that falls in the very center to be at least the same size as the cover so that everything holds together well. Cut a strip of paper the same length as the cover and fold it in half to make a hole-punching template. Use a ruler to mark $1/2$" (12mm) from the top and bottom, then make marks 1" (3cm) from the $1/2$" (12mm) marks, alternating from the top and bottom, until you reach the center (the section may be slightly larger than the others—that's okay). Draw a small arrow to indicate the top of the template. (See the diagram below.)

PUNCHING TEMPLATE

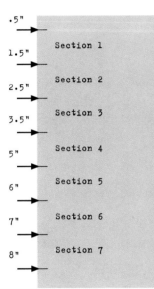

.5"
Section 1
1.5"
Section 2
2.5"
Section 3
3.5"
Section 4
5"
Section 5
6"
Section 6
7"
Section 7
8"

6. PUNCH THE HOLES

Place the template inside the pages and use a binder clip to secure it. Use an awl to punch holes at each of the marks, then remove the template.

7. SEW THE SIGNATURE

Measure waxed linen thread three times the length of the signature. Start sewing at the inside bottom hole and push the needle through to the outside. Leave a few inches (several centimeters) of loose thread at the bottom. Keep stitching to the top of the pages, then sew back down to the bottom, going through the holes in the opposite direction.

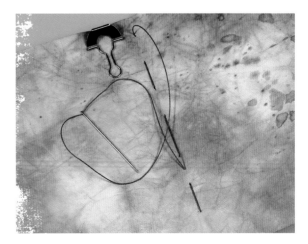

8. SEW SIGNATURES INTO THE COVER

Sew back through the last stitch and make a knot at the hole on the outside cover. Open the book and make a knot on the inside hole, with the other piece of loose thread.

9. COMPLETE FIVE SIGNATURES

Repeat steps 1–8 until you have five signatures.

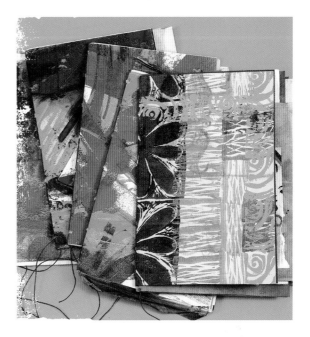

10. BIND THE SIGNATURES

Measure thread six times the length of the signatures. Thread the needle and pull it through the top stitch of the first signature, and tie a knot to secure it. Clip a second signature to the back of the first, using a binder clip. Insert the needle from the back of the second signature through the top stitch, then through the top stitch of the first signature. To complete the binding, see the techniques on pages 86–90 for options.

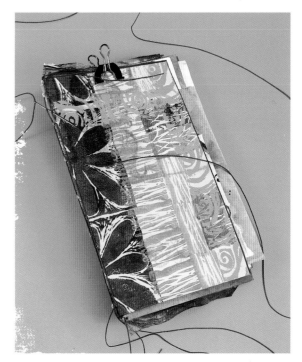

Now that you know how to create basic signatures, let me share with you several fun ways to bind everything together. All of the following binding techniques are meant to add interesting texture to the spine of your book or journal. There really is no "wrong" way to complete these bindings, as long as your technique holds the signatures together. Have fun experimenting and adding your own funky twist to each technique.

CREATIVE TOOLBOX

PRE-SEWN SIGNATURES, READY TO BIND

WAXED LINEN THREAD

ASSORTED BEADS

PAPER SEWING NEEDLES

HEMP TWINE

STRIPS OF FABRIC, YARN, FIBER OR RIBBON

TAPESTRY NEEDLE

CROCHET HOOK

SEWING MACHINE

LATCH HOOK CANVAS

free-form bead macramé

A blast from the past, this binding is actually the half-hitch stitch in traditional macramé. Each signature of a book is sewn separately and then bound together using the macramé stitch. By altering the number of strands of waxed linen, the size of the bead or embellishment, and the styles of tying off the ends, you can create a variety of different looks with one stitch!

1. BEGIN TYING KNOTS

With the length of linen threads still untrimmed on the signatures, tie one knot, then repeat three or four more times, until you reach the center of the stitch. Thread a bead on the thread. The next knot is the same; only this time, there is a bead on the thread.

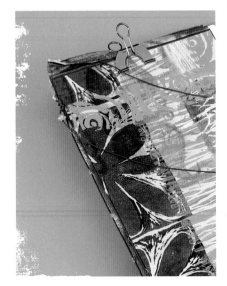

2. TIE TO BOTTOM

Continue the tying with three or four knots and repeat, until you reach the bottom of the signature.

1. ANOTHER OPTION

A variation of this technique: Tie a separate piece of thread to the top of the next pair of stitches. You will need a needle on each thread. Thread the needles through the previous stitches in opposite directions, tying a knot with each stitch.

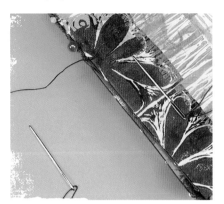

2. THREAD BEAD

After several stitches, run both threads through a bead and continue knotting.

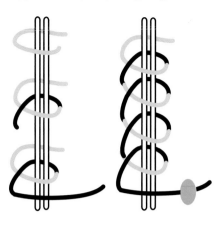

woven hemp

A simple woven binding looks fabulous and can vary greatly, depending on the type of fiber or string used. Experiment with hemp cord, twine or thin strips of fabric as variations to this technique. You can use the same waxed thread that you used to sew the signatures for this technique, or you can use jute, decorative fibers or anything else that you can get through a tapestry needle.

1. SECURE SIGNATURES

Create four signatures (see steps 1–8 on pages 83–85) and secure them together with a binder clip at the top.

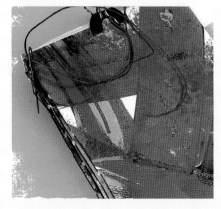

2. WEAVE CORD THROUGH SIGNATURES

Measure cord or twine three times the length of the signatures. Start sewing as in step 10 on page 85. Then weave the cord over and under the binding of each signature, pulling tautly as you go. Weave back in the opposite direction and repeat down the whole spine.

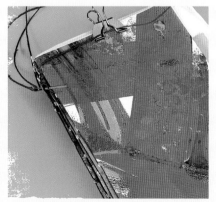

WOVEN HEMP BINDING

waxed linen on signature
fabric or fiber woven through signatures

knotted fabric

This is a super-easy technique that you can do with strips of any type of fabric, yarn or fibers. I like the strips to be a bit frayed looking.

FILL SPINE WITH KNOTS

Another way to bind the signatures together is to simply run short strips of fabric or ribbon under the threads and tie a knot. Fold each strip of fabric in half width-wise. Thread it onto a tapestry needle and push it through two of the threads that bind each signature so that a loop of fabric is on one side of the threads and two loose ends of fabric are on the other. Pull the loose ends through the loop and tighten. Repeat this for the next two threads, so there will be two knots side by side. Keep repeating until you've filled the entire spine with shaggy, knotted fabric.

idea

As a variation, you can use a tapestry needle and thin strips of fabric and leave tails hanging as you sew down the binding. You can change from one fabric or fiber to another, often, to create a fringy binding.

free-form crochet binding

Freestyle crochet creates a random, textured and colorful binding to embellish journals or purses. By using different chain lengths and connecting them randomly, you can really have some fun. The beauty is that you don't need a pattern and there is no right or wrong. The directions given here are just an example. To use on a book binding, tie a piece of yarn to a sewn section of waxed linen on a signature and start to crochet. I like using a very large hook (size Q) because I like the loose look of the large holes.

Cast on a stitch. Chain 16 and slip a stitch through the fifth stitch. Chain 10 and slip a stitch through the middle of the last chain. Chain 12 and pick up a stitch anywhere on the chain and slip a stitch. Chain 10, slip a stitch through any chain, chain 15 . . . you get the hang of it. Continue working until you are satisfied with the piece. Hang tags or beads at the end(s) of your fiber.

machine stitch binding

You've seen how your sewing machine can be used as a "painting" tool to create flowers and cool free-form stitching (and there's more to come on page 91), but it's also very practical for binding signatures. This is super-quick and easy.

STITCH ALONG FOLD

Take your folded signatures and open them to the center on top of the inside book cover. Run a straight stitch with a wide length over the center of the signatures. Make sure you do not use a short stitch length; this will cause your pages to perforate.

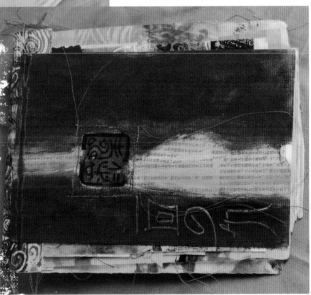

latch and rug hook binding

This is a twist on a technique that I used to do when I was a little girl creating all those latch-hooked rugs. Instead of yarn, I use strips of fabric, ribbons and fibers to create this fantastic fabric binding bursting from the spine!

LATCH HOOK BINDING

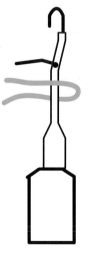 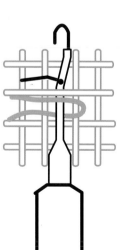 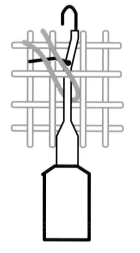 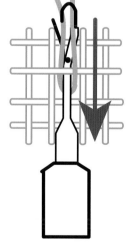 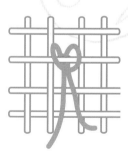

embellishing with stitches

Here are some of my favorite machine stitching techniques.
Use the sampler on page 122 as a guide to practice sewing.

funky straight stitching

Use a sewing machine set on a straight stitch
with a long stitch length. Sew a few stitches,
then press the reverse button and stitch a few
more. Release the reverse and continue stitching
forward. Do this along the edge of fabric or
paper. You can also use a contrasting thread
color to highlight areas of painted designs.

free-form flowers

Using a sewing machine set on either
a zigzag stitch or a long-length
straight stitch, I sew freeform
floral designs on my journal covers and hand-painted fabric pieces
by moving the fabric back and forth
through the machine and using the
reverse button to create my designs.
There is no planning in advance—
I take a piece of fabric and just
sew. I have included a few designs
that you can use as a guide to
create your very own flowers.
Photocopy the floral templates
and practice stitching on paper,
transfer the floral shapes to a piece
of fabric, or use a disappearing pen
to draw your design on the fabric.

wild zigzag stitching

Using a sewing machine set on a zigzag stitch, start to sew the largest
zigzag stitch with the stitch length set very low (I usually set it to .5
on my machine). This will create zigzag stitches that are very close to
each other. As you sew, alter the stitch width by moving the lever back and
forth to change the size of the zigzag as you go. Make sure to follow the
manufacturer's instructions when using your machine.

Here are a variety of stitches that I like to incorporate into my work. Be free, let your machine move wildly and randomly, pulling the fabric back and forth as you use the reverse lever. Use these as a visual guide or photocopy them and use them as actual patterns to practice sewing on paper. I have also provided stitching guides for you to photocopy on page 122.

before we move on

I am so inspired by creative binding and embellishment options, and I'm continually finding new ways to finish off my books, journals and art. Here are more super-easy ways to give your own work a creative edge!

FUNKY EMBROIDERY

"Painting" with thread and beads is another great way to add detail to the edge of your journal covers or to highlight an area on a painted piece of fabric. Here are a few of my favorite funky handstitches.

CHAIN STITCH

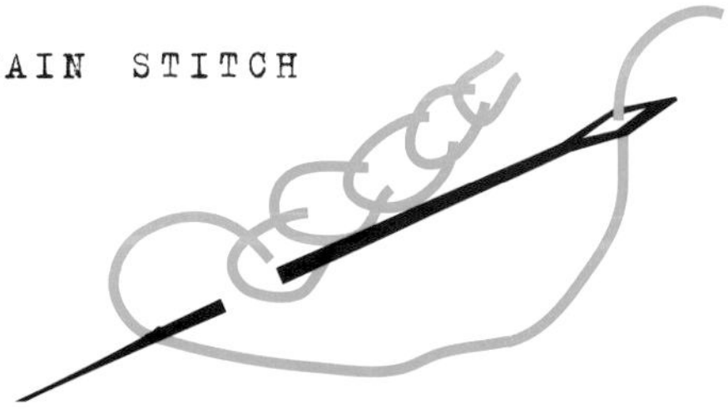

BLANKET STITCH

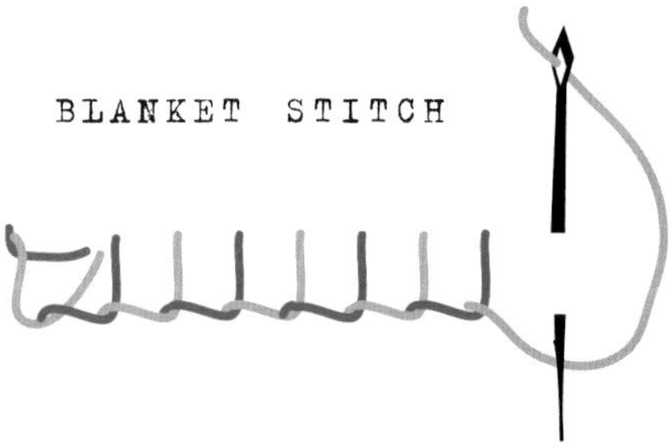

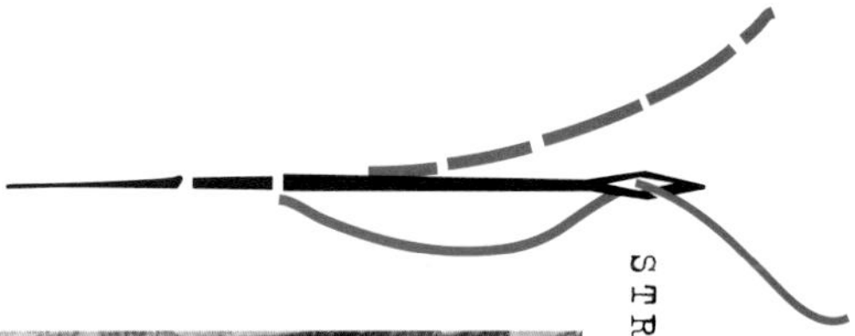

STRAIGHT STITCH

COOL EMBELLISHMENTS

I'd like to share four final embellishment ideas with you before we move on.
Metal is the primary ingredient in these embellishments, which contrasts nicely with paper and fabric.

Doodles in craft metal

Draw or doodle designs onto a piece of silver craft metal with a ballpoint pen or stylus. Rub over the top of the embossed design with india ink to give it a distressed look. Use nail polish to add metallic color.

Metal tags, fabric and transparencies

To create tag embellishments, take a piece of thin colored sheet metal and cut it into the size of the tag. Cut a piece of hand-painted paper or fabric and a word transparency to size and place them on top of the metal. Fold over the edges of the sheet metal, and hammer to set.

Wire beading

Punch holes at the edge of a book cover or craft metal sheet, and wire-wrap 22-gauge wire through the holes, adding beads as you go.

Stapling and riveting

Another fast and easy way to attach papers or photos to a collage or book cover is with colored staples, rivets or eyelets.

imagine

Soul diva

unLeaShed

PROJECTS *combining techniques*

The time has come for you to unleash your desire to play and create freely!

Now that you have seen how easy it is to make your mark and create wonderful, interesting layers of painted paper, transparencies and fabric, it's time to dig in and make something that is a true reflection of you.

This final chapter combines all of the techniques that I have shared with you. You'll see how you can use all the creative ways to paint, stitch and bind your works of art together to create fun and funky art journals, a wall hanging and even a jumbo tote bag. As with all of the techniques in the previous chapters, there are no rules with these projects; I simply wanted to show you how far you can take them to create wonderful works of your own, and to give you an inspirational place to start. No two pieces will ever look alike because we all approach art and play differently, with different colors, textures and imagery. I hope I've encouraged you to let loose and abandon any fears you may have previously had about expressing yourself. Never lose the child inside of you and remember to create for one reason and for one person—it's FUN and it's for YOU.

play.dream.explore.create!

gRaffiti Wall

By creating with no fear, an edgy
style and many layers, you will free
your art spirit. Combine fusion-dyed
collage, painting and staining paper,
monoprints, and freestyle lettering
and doodling to create a large canvas.
Visual journal paintings layered with
black-and-white images, expressive
sumi marks, spray-painted letters,
symbols, letterforms and written words
make up this unique work. Inspired
by the juxtaposition of colorful urban
graffiti walls and freestyle calligraphy, you will unleash your creative
ideas as you work big and write large
to create multiple-layered collages
with extreme, vibrant color, texture
and raw edges.

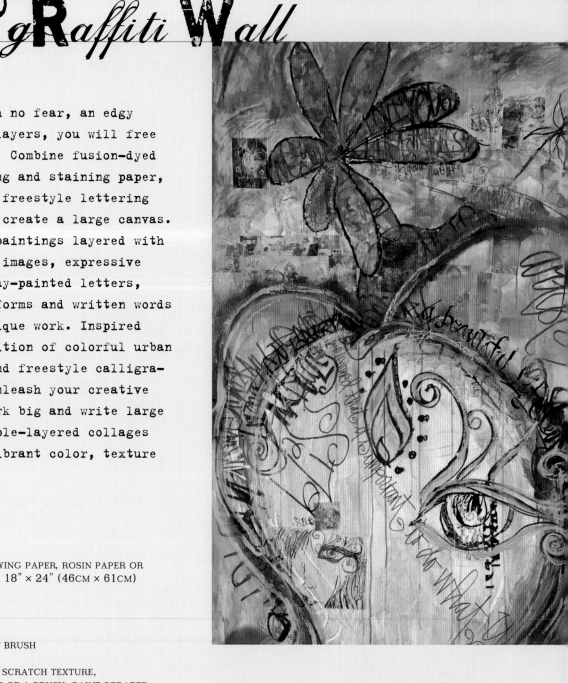

CREATIVE TOOLBOX

HEAVY-WEIGHT DRAWING PAPER, ROSIN PAPER OR
WATERCOLOR PAPER, 18" × 24" (46CM × 61CM)
OR LARGER

GESSO

2-INCH (51MM) FLAT BRUSH

ASSORTED TOOLS TO SCRATCH TEXTURE,
SUCH AS THE HANDLE OF A BRUSH, PAINT SCRAPER,
SKEWER AND SO ON

LARGE CHISEL-TIP BLACK PERMANENT MARKER

BLACK-AND-WHITE LASER PHOTOCOPIES OF JOURNAL
PAGES, DOODLES OR OTHER IMAGES

GEL MEDIUM

DYED PAPER TOWELS (SEE PAGE 10)

FLUID ACRYLICS, THINNED WITH WATER

FOAM BRUSH

HEAVY-BODIED ACRYLICS

ASSORTED TOOLS TO STAMP TEXTURE,
SUCH AS RUBBER STAMPS, STENCILS,
TEXTURED WALLPAPER AND SO ON

SPRAY PAINT

GLITTER DIMENSIONAL PAINT

WHITEOUT PEN

Washes

Doodles

1. LAY DOWN GESSO

Apply gesso to the surface of the large drawing paper, using the flat brush. Scratch textures into the surface and let dry.

2. WRITE WITH MARKER

Write words, freestyle letters and doodles over the top of the dried gesso with a chisel-tip black permanent marker.

3. ADD PHOTOCOPIES

Using a flat brush and gel medium, layer on black-and-white laser photocopies.

4. LAYER PAPER TOWELS

Layer dyed paper towels over the black-and-white photocopies with gel medium.

5. LAY DOWN A WASH

Wash watered-down paints over the top of the black-and-white art, letting the paint drip by loading paint on a very damp brush. Wash on two or three colors of paint.

6. ADD TEXTURE

Accent the washed design by painting with heavy-bodied acrylics. Stamp in textures, stencil designs and create patterns with rubber stamps.

7. USE SPRAY PAINT

Add a few sprays of paint with a spray paint can.

8. FINISH WITH HIGHLIGHTS

Add sparkle with glitter dimensional paint, and write over the top of the canvas with a whiteout pen.

99

idea!

Optional items for play
- Paint markers, pens and pencils—Spider Writers, gel pen markers, large-nib calligraphy pens (I use the 15mm), Sharpie chisel-tip permanent markers, colored pencils
- Images—black-and-white photocopies of photos, writing, journal pages and personal images. Large patterns, symbols and letters work best. TIP: Enlarge images on the copy machine to blow up into the backgrounds for collage.
- Unmounted deeply etched rubber stamps
- Heat gun (to speed drying time between layers

Freestyle lettering

Fusion-dyed collage

plaY aRt journal

Be inspired by color. Vibrant, playful, inspirational, unique . . . these words describe the creative process for creating this whimsical art piece. Assemble a beautiful, one-of-a-kind artist's journal with a funky beaded macramé binding and collaged canvas covers. You will begin by creating hand-painted signature pages; then you will assemble the book signatures using a mélange of hand-painted papers and found papers.

100

CREATIVE TOOLBOX

PIECES OF CARDSTOCK OR CANVAS THAT HAVE BEEN PAINTED AND COLOR SCRAPED (SEE PAGE 12), FIVE TO SEVEN TOTAL

EXTRA CARDSTOCK OR FABRIC FOR BACKING THE

COLOR-SCRAPED PIECES

PVA OR CRAFT GLUE

ADHESIVE SPREADER

COLLECTION OF PAPERS FOR SIGNATURES
(SEE IDEA LIST, THIS PAGE), THIRTY TO FIFTY TOTAL

BONE FOLDER

RULER

AWL

WAXED LINEN OR HEMP CORD

SCISSORS

PAPER NEEDLE

BEADS (OPTIONAL)

EMBELLISHMENTS
(BEADS, CHARMS, ACRYLIC TAGS AND SO ON)

idea!

Consider these options for collecting found papers for your journal signatures.

Vellum	Catalog pages	Maps
Napkins	Photocopied images	Wallpaper samples
Ledger paper	Dictionary pages	Paint chips
Graph paper	Old book pages	Ribbons
Envelopes	Fabric	Doilies
Joss paper	Tissue paper	Computer paper
Hand-painted paper	Brown bags	Newspaper
Handmade paper	Tyvek envelopes	Comics
Magazine pages	Receipts	Paper bags

1. MOUNT COVERS TO CARDSTOCK

Back the painted covers with another piece of cardstock or fabric to make them sturdier. Spread adhesive from the middle of the paper and extend over all edges. This is an important step to make sure the edges don't lift. (See page 83.)

2. ORGANIZE SIGNATURES AND PUNCH HOLES

Fold assorted papers in half; these will become the folios of the signatures. Use a bone folder to burnish the fold. Decide which pages you want in each signature and stack them together. Place each stack inside a painted collaged cover. I recommend five to fifteen pages per signature, depending on the thickness of the papers. Punch evenly spaced holes in the spine of each signature with an awl. Punch six to nine holes, depending on the height of the pages. (See Creating Signatures on page 82.)

3. STITCH INDIVIDUAL SIGNATURES

For each signature, measure waxed linen three times the length of the spine and cut. Thread needle. Sewing with a single thread, start from the inside bottom hole, pull the thread through the hole and leave a 3" (8cm) tail. Sew a running straight stitch all the way to the top, then back down the signature until both strings are hanging from the bottom holes. Tie off each signature at the bottom hole with a square knot. Continue until all signatures are sewn. Leave the bottom outside threads; they will be tied together at each signature to make the binding sturdier. Bead or tie knots in additional threads on the outside of the signature. Place all signatures in the binding order.

4. SEW FIRST THREE SIGNATURES TOGETHER

Measure waxed linen six times the length of the spine and cut. Thread needle and tie off the thread onto the top section of the first signature. Take the first two signatures and bind the first and second signatures together at section 1 (the first, top stitches) with a square macramé knot. (See free-form bead macramé binding on page 86.) Then add the third signature and bind the second and third signatures at section 2 (the second stitches, down). Go back to the first and second signatures and bind at section 3. Then, with the second and third signatures, bind at section 4. Repeat, and continue to bind zigzag down the spine of all three signatures. (See chart for joining signatures, this page.)

5. CONTINUE JOINING SIGNATURES

Add fourth, fifth signature and so on, with the same square knot.

6. ADD EMBELLISHMENTS

Add beads, charms, keys, acrylic tags, painted dominoes, or any embellishments of your choice in the middle of the stitch on each section and to the tails of the leftover waxed linen. Add beads to the tails at the bottom of the signatures.

Painted canvas papers

Freeform bead macramé

1 2 3 4 5

←add beads to end of strings

Variations

Inside signatures

102

Create a journal with patchwork-art-quilt covers combining altered paper, transparencies and hand-painted cloth. Explore fabric and paper painting and dyeing techniques, including color scraping, monoprints, dyed cloth stamping and stenciling, and glazing. Doodle letters and faces on fabric, layer fabric with hand-painted transparencies and color-dyed images. Adorn fabric collage patches with my version of funky freestyle stitching techniques. The hand-painted signatures are made up of random-sized pages interlaced with found papers and photocopies of original artwork. The spine is embellished with freeform macramé, crochet and beads.

CREATIVE TOOLBOX

FABRIC-PAPER PATCHWORK COLLAGE, FOR TWO JOURNAL COVERS (SEE PAGE 72)

SEWING MACHINE

RAYON THREAD FOR MACHINE NEEDLE

COTTON THREAD FOR BOBBIN

COLOR COPIES OF ARTWORK

TRANSPARENCIES

ASSORTED RIBBON AND FABRIC SCRAPS

PAINTED PAPER FLOWERS

ASSORTED PAPERS FOR SIGNATURES (HAND-PAINTED/DYED PAPERS, FOUND PAPERS, BLACK-AND-WHITE OR COLOR PHOTOCOPIES AND SO ON)

METAL CORK-BACKED RULER

BONE FOLDER

AWL

WAXED LINEN THREAD

PAPER NEEDLE

TAPESTRY NEEDLES

EMBELLISHMENTS (BEADS, CHARMS, ACRYLIC TAGS)

ASSORTED FIBERS

CROCHET HOOK, SIZE Q

1. ADD TRANSPARENCIES AND STITCHING TO COVER

Add a free-form stitch of a floral design to your patchwork cover, using a sewing machine threaded with rayon thread. Attach color copies and transparencies with random straight and zigzag stitches. Layer transparencies over pieces of ribbon or fabric and stitch to the fabric collage. Stitch on painted paper flowers over the fabric. Finish off the edge of the journal cover with a zigzag stitch, letting the edges of fabric hang off the edges of the covers.

103

Free-form crochet and macramé

Painted fabric patches

2. COMPLETE COVER QUILT

Repeat similar embellishing as in step 1 to make a back cover, and attach the two by grafting them together with a wide zigzag stitch to create the spine. I like to use silence cloth as a padded backing between the covers.

3. FOLD SIGNATURE PAGES

Tear the assorted papers into random-sized pieces against a metal cork-backed ruler. Fold pages. I fold my papers to a variety of lengths, so the papers are randomly sized. Place eight to twelve folded pages together to form a signature. On pages that are short after they're folded, sew on additional small papers with a zigzag stitch to extend them. Create three signatures.

4. MACHINE STITCH SIGNATURES TOGETHER

Place one signature into the spine, and machine stitch with a straight stitch. Make sure the stitch length is long or the papers will perforate. Continue to add each signature next to the previous one and machine stitch into the spine. Or, if you wish, you can hand-stitch the signatures into the spine.

Funky embroidery and free-form stitching

5. APPLY MACRAMÉ STITCHING

Measure waxed linen thread three times the length of the spine. Use the paper needle to sew the signatures into the spine, starting at the inside bottom. Continue with a running straight stitch up the spine, then back down the spine. Embellish the outside stitch lengths with free-form bead macramé stitches and freestyle crochet fibers. (See Funky Binding Techniques on pages 86–88.)

Note: The stitching in this step is for decorative purposes only, because the signatures are already secured to the spine from the sewing machine. Leaving the spine free of the macramé or free-style crochet stitches provides an entirely new look and may be one you prefer.

Metal tag and bead embellishments

Stained and dyed papers

Wanderlust: a strong impulse to move about without a fixed course or aim; the longing to travel. Begin by creating painted canvas covers and hand-painted signature pages. The book signatures are a mélange of found papers, including file folders, postcards, graph paper, watercolor paper, napkins, maps, vellums, transparencies, tags and envelopes. Create a place to wander through as you journal and keep a collection of your daily thoughts and travels. This beautiful one-of-a-kind artist's journal is bound with a woven fiber binding.

104

CREATIVE TOOLBOX

PIECES OF CARDSTOCK OR CANVAS THAT HAVE BEEN COLOR SCRAPED (SEE PAGE 12), FIVE TO SEVEN TOTAL

EXTRA CARDSTOCK OR FABRIC FOR BACKING THE COLOR-SCRAPED PIECES

PVA OR THINNED CRAFT GLUE

ADHESIVE SPREADER

COLLECTION OF PAPERS FOR SIGNATURES (SEE IDEA LIST, PAGE 100)

BONE FOLDER

AWL

WAXED LINEN THREAD

SCISSORS

PAPER NEEDLE

BINDER CLIP

FIBERS (¼" [6MM] RIBBON, STRIPS OF FABRIC, TWINE, CRAFT STRING, RAFFIA AND SO ON)

TAPESTRY NEEDLE

LARGE-HOLED BEADS (OPTIONAL)

idea!

Collect various paper items from a vacation and bind them to create a travel journal of your trip! Here are some canvas cover ideas for this or any other journal:

- Collage on a funky face with random collage items
- Collage on dictionary pages
- Stain covers with sepia-toned varnish for a vintage antique look
- Stamp with interference gold ink for a hint of color
- Stamp with black StazOn for a permanent contrasted image
- Write over acrylics with paint pens, galaxy markers, or parallel pens
- Use india ink in an eyedropper to create flowing marks, flowers and faces
- Use rub-on letters for words
- Add stickers
- Do a tape resist with your paints

Color-scraped covers

Woven fiber binding

1. MOUNT COVERS TO CARDSTOCK

Back the painted covers with another piece of cardstock or fabric to create sturdier covers. Spread adhesive from the middle of the paper, extending over all edges. This is an important step to make sure the edges don't lift.

2. FOLD PAPERS

Fold thirty to fifty pages (see list of paper ideas on page 100) in half; these will become the folios of the signatures. Decide which pages you want in each signature and stack them together.

3. ASSEMBLE SIGNATURES

Fold painted/collaged canvas covers in half. Place signature pages inside the covers. Punch seven evenly spaced holes in the spine of each signature with an awl.

4. SEW SIGNATURES

For each signature, measure waxed linen thread three times the length of the spine and cut. Thread the paper needle and sew a straight stitch starting from the inside bottom hole all the way to the top, then back down the signature until both strings are hanging from the bottom. Tie off each signature with a square knot.

5. TIE ON FIBERS

Place sewn signatures in order. Take the first fiber and tie it off at the top of the first signature and weave it through each of the other signatures (under and over each string of waxed linen), with the tapestry needle. Continue weaving fiber, ribbon or string in and out of each signature. Add each new fiber by tying it onto the waxed linen, and continue weaving until you reach the bottom. Change fibers frequently to create a binding that has many variations in color and texture.

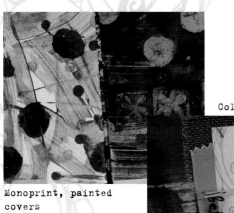

Monoprint, painted covers

Collaged canvas

idea!

I like to add Asian silk brocade fabrics to my books—glorious! Here are some funky ideas for binding with fibers that might get you going:

- Use a rotary cutter to cut up fabric into 1/4" to 1/2" (6mm to 12mm) wide strips, 12" to 15" (30cm to 38cm) in length
- Use ribbon and fibers with funky textures
- Hand-dye white textured fabrics and cut into strips, then add beads, charms or trinkets
- Hot glue small silk flowers onto ribbons
- Sew canvas letters onto hanging strings
- Use acrylic tags as accents
- Make handmade or hand-painted beads to add to hanging fibers
- Make mini art quilted pieces to hang from fibers
- Use beads with large holes (they are easier to string on thicker fabric pieces and textured fibers)
- Alternate fiber and ribbon with different colors and textures
- Look for fabrics that have glorious color, fun patterns and great texture to cut up
- Look at fabric with a different eye: When you look for fabric for this project, think about the pattern you will see when it is cut up into 1/4" (6mm) strips
- Look for vintage ribbon and trims; they make great accents

The word "ruins" conjures images of crumbling cities and ancient stone walls. That feeling is captured by using metallic colors and found papers. This book is the perfect final resting place for left-overs from past projects. The faux metallic cover and random-sized pages are fusion-dyed layers of found papers—stained, deconstructed, texturized and layered with collage, images and words. Accents of embellished metals finish off the pages, bound with a beaded binding.

CREATIVE TOOLBOX

HOT-PRESS WATERCOLOR PAPER 5½" × 30" (14CM × 76CM)

METALLIC CRAYONS OR CRAYON CUPCAKES (SEE PAGE 15)

TRAVEL IRON WITHOUT HOLES

DYED TWO-PLY PAPER TOWELS, TEN TOTAL

PVA OR THINNED CRAFT GLUE

2-INCH (51MM) FLAT BRUSH

METAL CORK-BACKED RULER

ASSORTED PAINTED AND COLLAGED PAPERS

BONE FOLDER

⅛" (3MM) EYELET SETTER AND PUNCH

EYELETS

STAPLES

TAPE

PHOTOS

TRANSPARENCIES

CRAFT HAMMER

AWL

WAXED LINEN THREAD

PAPER NEEDLE

ASSORTED BEADS AND ACRYLIC TAGS

Fusion-dyed collage pages

1. COVER WATERCOLOR PAPER

Using the Painting With Crayons technique on page 16, cover one or both sides of the water-color paper with crayon melt.

2. MAKE MINI-DYED COLLAGES

Create mini fusion-dyed collage pages (5$^1/2$" x 7" [14cm x 18cm]) by layering single plies of the towels with PVA, using a flat brush. (See Transparent Technique, page 62.)

3. FOLD WATERCOLOR PAPER

Divide the dyed watercolor paper into two 5$^1/2$" x 9" (14cm x 23cm) pieces and four 5$^1/2$" x 3" (14cm x 8cm) pieces, by tearing the paper using a metal ruler. Fold the 3" (8cm) pieces in half; these become the flaps for each signature. Fold the larger pieces to 5$^1/2$" x 7" (14cm x 18cm), so there is a 2" (5cm) flap on each cover piece.

4. ADHERE PIECES TO FLAPS

Create signatures by attaching assorted fusion-dyed collage pieces, transparencies, photos and painted papers to the flaps. Attach everything using a combination of eyelets, staples and tape. Full collage pages can be attached to the shorter flaps.

5. PUNCH HOLES

Punch five evenly spaced holes into the fold of each signature. Measure out a piece of waxed linen thread three times the length of the book. Sew a single strand of waxed linen with a paper needle, beginning at the inside bottom hole. Continue with a running stitch all the way up the book, and then repeat until you have a piece of waxed linen coming out of both sides of the bottom holes.

6. APPLY MACRAMÉ STITCH

Use a funky macramé stitch to bind the signatures. (See Free-form Bead Macramé on page 86.)

7. EMBELLISH WITH BEADS

Embellish the ends of the threads with assorted beads and acrylic tags.

Transparency-washed photocopy collage

Transparencies

Staples and tape collage

Transparency-tape collage

coLoring Book

Paint. Dye. Collage. Stitch. Create a colorful "idea" book with sewn random-sized, dyed pages interlaced with found papers. This book is perfect for just one, two or three signatures. The cover is a fusion-dyed collage layered with color-dyed images and stitched designs. Explore my favorite color-dyeing techniques for black-and-white images using paints and pens. Play with creative lettering and doodles on images and transparencies using colored pencils, oil pastels, gel pens, glitter paint writers, sumi ink and eyedroppers.

idea!

This book is highly suitable to a variety of bindings such as the knotted fabric, free-form macramé, wire or stick bindings.

FUSION-DYED COLLAGE ON DELI PAPER, 12" × 12" (30CM × 30CM) (SEE LAYERING OVER IMAGES, PAGE 63)

FOAM BRUSH

METALLIC PAINT PENS

STENCILS

ACRYLIC PAINTS

SEWING MACHINE, THREADED WITH RAYON THREAD (COTTON THREAD IN THE BOBBIN)

ASSORTED TRANSPARENCIES

FLUID ACRYLICS, THINNED WITH WATER

2-INCH (51MM) FLAT BRUSH

ASSORTMENT OF LASER-COPIED GIRLIE GLAM DOODLES (PAGE 123)

COLLECTION OF PAPERS FOR SIGNATURES, INCLUDING HAND-PAINTED AND DYED PAPERS (SEE IDEA LIST, PAGE 100)

METAL CORK-BACKED RULER

Assorted sizes of
signature pages

1. ACCENT COLLAGE WITH PAINT PENS

Accent the top of the collaged cover by painting through stencils, using a foam brush and adding doodled letters and words with metallic paint pens.

Freestyle stitching

2. ATTACH TRANSPARENCIES

Add funky free-form machine stitching by altering stitch lengths using a zigzag and straight stitch. Stitch around shapes with a contrasting thread color. Attach transparencies and images with a machine stitch. Variation: Attach a piece of hand-painted paper or color copy of artwork to cover the back of the fusion-dyed collage.

3. ADD IMAGE INSIDE THE COVERS

To finish off the inside covers of the book, machine stitch a color laser or hand-painted paper to the front cover using a zigzag stitch to finish off the edge. I usually piece together a couple of different pieces of paper for the inside cover.

4. COLOR PHOTOCOPY

Color in a photocopy of the "girlie glam" images (see page 51) using various pens and markers. After it is dry, attach it to the cover of the book. Don't worry if your stitching shows through to the inside cover; it adds to the handmade quality and richness of the book's design.

Lettering and doodling

5. CREATE SIGNATURE

To create a signature, use the metal ruler to tear random-sized pages that will fit into the book when it is folded in half (6" × 12" [15cm × 30cm]). I use a variety of painted and stained papers, found papers, ledger paper and yellow writing paper, and I include photocopies of my original artwork. Fold the pages and layer each folded page on top of the next to create one signature. I use eight to fifteen pages per signature, depending on the thickness of the paper.

6. STITCH SIGNATURE TOGETHER

Fold your fusion-dyed collage cover in half and place the folded signature in the center of the cover. Machine stitch using a long machine stitch, being careful not to perforate the paper. Add another signature next to the first if you want a larger book.

Stamping

Stitching transparencies

109

Create a retro quilted journal inspired by treasure hunts through thrift stores. The patchwork art quilts are created with hand-painted cloths combined with fabric and embellishments from vintage finds such as jeans . . . Hawaiian muumuus . . . 70s T-shirts . . . scarves and funky costume jewelry. The binding is the retro technique of rug hooking with a twist, using fabric, fibers and ribbons. Use a variation of this technique to create a wall hanging or a handbag!

110

idea!

Places to look for finding vintage items:

- ✿ Look at vintage clothing for patterns and what you can cut out of them.
- ✿ Look for pieces that have interesting embellishments (lace, buttons, patches).
- ✿ Look for belts with funky designs or buckles.
- ✿ Look for Hawaiian muumuus or housecoats; they have beautiful, bright colors and funky patterns.
- ✿ Use buttons from old shirts.
- ✿ Use charms and beads from vintage jewelry and necklaces, and buckles from purses and wallets.
- ✿ Look for latch hooks and crochet hooks at the thrift stores—you might get them for $.20 to $1.00.
- ✿ Cut pockets out of clothing items and sew them into your art quilts.

CREATIVE TOOLBOX

COLOR-SCRAPED AND HAND-PAINTED FABRICS (SEE PAGE 12)

VINTAGE TREASURES (OLD BELTS, SCARVES, FABRIC PIECES, BUTTONS)

PVA, CRAFT GLUE OR FUSIBLE WEB

ASSORTED FABRICS (MUSLIN, KONA COTTON, PRE-QUILTED MUSLIN, CANVAS)

SILENCE CLOTH

SEWING MACHINE, THREADED WITH RAYON THREAD

ASSORTMENT OF LASER-COPIED GIRLIE GLAMS

DOODLES (SEE PAGE 123) (COLOR AND BLACK-AND-WHITE)

ASSORTED TRANSPARENCIES

ASSORTED PENS (GEL, MARKERS, CRAYOLA SPIDER WRITERS, PAINT)

LATCH HOOK CANVAS

FABRIC SCISSORS

LATCH HOOK

CROCHET HOOK, SIZE 6

EMBROIDERY FLOSS, FIBERS

FABRIC STRIPS (¼" TO ½" [6MM TO 13MM] PRE-CUT STRIPS)

EMBROIDERY NEEDLES AND ASSORTED THREADS

EMBELLISHMENTS (BEADS, FIBERS, FABRIC, WIRE, CHARMS, LETTER TILES, RIBBON, SILK FLOWERS, MEMENTOS, ACRYLIC TAGS)

1. CREATE TWO JOURNAL COVERS

Combine color-scraped and hand-painted fabrics with scraps from vintage treasures to create two fabric patchwork collage art quilts, using the "glue-as-you-go" method (see page 72), and PVA or craft glue. Attach the quilts to silence cloth by stitching funky free-form straight stitch and zigzag designs.

2. FINISH OFF EDGES

Free-form stitch on a floral design and attach color lasers and transparencies with random straight and zigzag stitches. Layer transparencies over pieces of ribbon or fabric and stitch to the fabric collage. Stitch on painted paper flowers over fabric. Finish off the edge of the art quilt with a zigzag stitch, letting edges of fabric hang off the edge.

3. ADD DOODLES

Write words and doodle over the top of the fabric with various gel pens, markers, Spider Writers and paint pens.

4. CREATE SIGNATURES

Create three to five signatures. (See Creating Signatures on page 82.) Once you have punched the holes in each signature, attach the signatures to a piece of heavy interfacing, using a strand of waxed linen and a paper needle. (See illustration, this page.)

5. CUT RUG HOOK CANVAS FOR SPINE

Cut a piece of rug hook canvas the same height as the fabric art quilt covers by about 4" (10cm) wide. Latch-hook a variety of fabric pieces, fibers and ribbons to canvas. Usually about five rows of the canvas is covered with fabric. (See illustration on this page.) Use the crochet hook to add free-form crochet to some of the fibers.

6. ADD INTERFACING

Insert the latch-hooked spine and the interfacing on the signatures into the edges of the journal covers. Sew or glue them together.

7. EMBELLISH WITH BEADS

Embellish the top of the journal cover by sewing on transparencies, buttons or beads, or adding funky embroidery stitches.

Bead embellishments

Funky embroidery

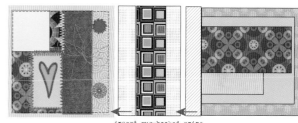

insert rug-hooked spine
between layers of art quilt

Colored doodles

Latch hook binding

Freestyle machine stitching, funky embroidery, free-form crochet, luscious, random stitching techniques. . . all are layered on painted, patchwork art quilts to create a funky large tote. The great thing about patchwork quilts is that you can alter them to create any shape or size you desire. This sack is big, but think about the possibilities—gift bags, knitting bags, book covers, backpacks . . .

CREATIVE TOOLBOX

ASSORTED HAND-PAINTED AND COLOR-SCRAPED FABRICS

ASSORTED PRINTED FABRIC SCRAPS

MUSLIN OR OTHER FABRIC FOR LINING (ENOUGH FOR BAG PATTERN)

FABRIC SCISSORS

IRON-ON ADHESIVE

PARCHMENT PAPER

IRON AND IRONING BOARD

SEWING MACHINE, THREADED WITH RAYON THREAD

ASSORTED BEADS

EMBROIDERY FLOSS AND NEEDLE

GRAFFITI-PRINTED FABRIC SCRAPS

VINTAGE BELT FOR HANDLE, OR ENOUGH FABRIC TO MAKE A HANDLE

1. PREPARE FABRICS

Create various hand-painted fabrics. (See Surface Designs on Fabric, page 20.)

2. CUT MUSLIN

Cut a piece of muslin to the size of the bag you want to design. (See design, this page.) Trace the pattern and cut out the bag shapes.

3. TEAR FABRIC INTO PIECES

Cut or tear your hand-painted and coordinating fabrics into various sizes. Adhere iron-on adhesive to the back of each fabric (follow package directions); remove paper backings and place onto muslin creating a collage of fabrics. Once you are satisfied with the composition cover it with parchment paper, then iron on the fabric to the muslin surface.

4. ACCENT WITH STITCHING AND EMBELLISHMENTS

Create a patchwork collage for the second side of the bag for variety, or you can create another iron-on collage. Accent the tops of the collages with free-form stitching, fabric printed with images and funky beaded embroidery.

5. ADD HANDLE

With right sides facing, sew together collage canvas pieces, then turn right side out. Create a bag handle with more fabric pieces sewn together, or use a vintage belt as the handle. Sew it to the bag.

6. ADD POCKET OR FLOWER

Variations: Add a latch-hooked patch on top of the bag, create a pocket on the outside of the bag, sew on transparencies or create a fabric collage flower. (See page 76.)

Painted fabric patches

Fabric strip collage

113

Freestyle floral stitched designs

Free-form crochet

Doodling & freestyle lettering on fabric

the aRtful wall

Create a wall of inspiration with fusion-dyed collages, mixed-media art quilts layered with dyed and painted papers and cloths accented with funky stitched designs and words. A simple wire technique is used to hang these fun collages. Apply the plethora of techniques you've learned in this book to create this hanging piece.

CREATIVE TOOLBOX

FABRIC-PAPER PATCHWORKS (SEE PAGE 72), THREE TO SEVEN TOTAL

⅛" (3MM) ANYWHERE PUNCH

⅛" (3MM) EYELETS

EYELET SETTER, CRAFT HAMMER AND MAT

18–20-GAUGE WIRE

ASSORTED BEADS

EMBROIDERY THREAD, WAXED LINEN OR OTHER FIBERS FOR EMBELLISHMENT

HEMP CORD

PICTURE-HANGING WIRE

idea!

◎ Make a wall hanging for the holidays using photos and cards from the year.
◎ Other theme ideas: baby's first year, winter, fashion, family, seasons, favorite things, color, pets or symbols.

1. ADD EYELETS

After creating your chosen number of patchwork collage quilts (see Fabric-Paper Patchwork Collage, page 72), set eyelets on the top and bottom of each quilted piece, using the anywhere punch, eyelet setter and a hammer.

2. CREATE WIRE HANGERS

Create a wire-beaded attachment by using 20-gauge wire and assorted beads. Fold the wire into an L shape, add a bead, thread it through an eyelet in another quilt piece, then fold the wire and wrap it around itself to complete. Create wire-wrapped beading for each quilt piece and connect to create wall hanging.

3. EMBELLISH WITH HEMP CORD

To create the wire hanger at the top, use picture-hanging wire. Make a free-form hanger shape by folding and twisting the wire until you are satisfied with the shape. Wrap the wire with embroidery thread and other fibers. Add beads to embellish. Add a piece of hemp cord and create a macramé design.

Wild zigzag stitching

Wire beading

Funky calligraphy/
freestyle lettering

Variation of
wire-beaded binding

Patchwork art quilts

Jewels of the East . . . this unique, handmade book is a collection of treasured personal images, papers and findings collected from my wanderings and travels through the open-air urban markets in Southeast Asia. The signatures are made up of gritty fusion-dyed collage covers layered with images and words. Experiment with interesting black-and-white art, made with sumi ink, photocopied patterns, handwritten text and symbols. Accents of distressed metals finish off the signatures of stained and texturized found papers that are bound with a funky, beaded macramé binding.

116

CREATIVE TOOLBOX

FUSION-DYED COLLAGE WORKS,
12" × 18" (30CM × 46CM) EACH, FIVE TOTAL

COLLECTION OF PAPERS FOR SIGNATURES
(SEE IDEA LIST, PAGE 100)

BONE FOLDER

METAL RULER

AWL

WAXED LINEN THREAD

PAPER NEEDLE

TAPESTRY NEEDLE

HEMP CORD, FIBERS (INDIAN SARI YARN)

EMBELLISHMENTS
(BEADS, FIBERS, FABRIC, CRAFT METAL, WIRE)

ASSORTED PENS
(GEL, MARKERS, CRAYOLA SPIDER WRITERS, PAINT PENS)

SEWING MACHINE, THREADED WITH RAYON THREAD

1. CREATE SIGNATURES

Create signatures using a fusion-dyed collage as a cover for each signature. Fold ten to fifteen painted or found papers (tear some of the papers down to size with a metal ruler) and use a bone folder to burnish the folds. Punch holes in the signatures with an awl and sew the signatures with waxed linen thread, using the paper needle (see Creating Signatures, page 82).

2. COMBINE BINDING TECHNIQUES

Bind together the signatures using a mixture of free-form bead macramé (see page 86) and woven hemp binding (see page 87), alternating fibers and hemp cord.

3. ACCENT WITH GRAFFITI

Add embellishments such as a doodled craft metal piece or wire-wrapped beading. Accent the covers with graffiti-style writing and machine stitching.

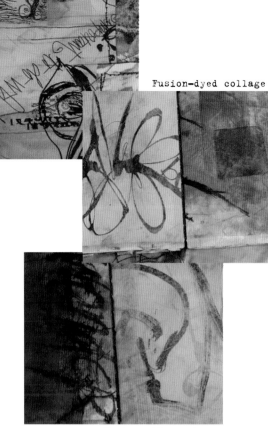

Doodling

Fusion-dyed collage

Funky calligraphy

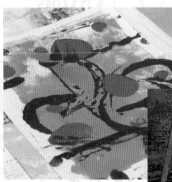

Stamping with
heavy-bodied acrylics

Dimensional glitter monoprint

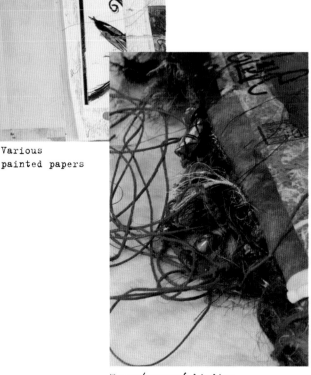

Various
painted papers

Woven/macramé binding

butterfly-Flower-graffiti Journal

Transformation. Bloom. Vibrant—bliss. No Rules. A mixture of natural beauty and urban street culture. Create a mixed-media journal with unconventional layers of textured painted papers, digital prints and fabrics covered with your own personal graffiti marks. The structure is sewn with a big, funky fabric flower collage, and signatures of random-sized stained papers are finished off with a freestyle mac-ramé binding. Make your mark accenting vibrant backgrounds with hand-made printing plates made from garden kneeling pads, cardboard, found objects and handmade stencils.

CREATIVE TOOLBOX

PAINTED AND COLOR-SCRAPED FABRICS AND PAPERS

DYED PAPER TOWELS, BACKED WITH IRON-ON INTERFACING

BROCADE AND SILK FABRICS

SILENCE CLOTH

SEWING MACHINE, THREADED WITH RAYON THREAD

FUSION-DYED COLLAGES, SIZED APPROPRIATELY FOR JOURNAL (AS MANY AS YOU LIKE— FOR MORE DETAILS, SEE PAGE 62.)

ASSORTED TRANSPARENCIES

BLACK-AND-WHITE PHOTOCOPIES OF FLORAL IMAGES

JOURNAL PAGES, MAGAZINE PAGES, FOUND PAPERS OR COLOR PRINTS OF IMAGES RELATED TO YOUR THEME

GESSO (STUDENT GRADE IS FINE)

FABRIC/PAPER SCISSORS

BONE FOLDER

METAL RULER

CRAFT GLUE

PAPER NEEDLE

SEWING/ EMBROIDERY NEEDLES

AWL

WAXED LINEN

INKJET IRON-ON FABRIC DESIGNS

EMBELLISHMENTS: BEADS, FIBERS, FABRIC, WIRE, CHARMS, LETTER TILES, RIBBON, SILK FLOWERS, MEMENTOS, ACRYLIC TAGS

1. BEGIN COVER

Combine color-scraped fabric with silk and brocade scraps, dyed paper towels and transparencies to create a fabric patchwork collage journal cover, using the sewing machine and silence cloth. (See page 72 for instruction on patchwork collage.)

2. COMPLETE PATCHWORK COLLAGE

Continue layering collage onto the cover: Free-form stitch on a floral design and attach color lasers and transparencies with random straight and zigzag stitches. Layer transparencies over pieces of ribbon or fabric and stitch them to the fabric collage. Stitch on painted paper flowers over the fabric. Stitch on iron-on fabric designs. Finish off the edge of the journal cover with a zigzag stitch, letting edges of fabric hang off the edge of the journal cover.

3. CREATE A CANVAS COLLAGE

For one or more of your signature covers, try creating a canvas collage with gesso texture and freestyle lettering. (See step 1, page 67.)

4. PREPARE SIGNATURE PAGES

Gather hand-painted papers and photocopies. Apply a thin layer of gesso over some of the photocopies to ghost the images. Fold the papers for signatures, using a ruler and a bone folder.

5. SANDWICH PHOTOCOPIES

Sandwich some of the black-and-white photocopies between two fusion-dyed collage papers; you should be able to see the photocopies through the collage. These will be used to back the covers and as inside pages.

6. ASSEMBLE JOURNAL

Assemble the signature pages. Create a template for punching holes and sew all of the signatures to the cover, using waxed linen thread and a paper needle. (See Creating Signatures, page 82.)

7. EMBELLISH BINDING

Embellish with a free-form macramé binding. Add beads and tags for extra embellishments. Weave assorted fibers through the tied binding, using a tapestry needle.

Freestyle lettering

Wild zigzag stitches

119

Free-form stitched flower

Freeform macramé binding

The goodies that appear on the following pages are here to encourage and inspire you in your own artful creations. Feel free to photocopy any of the images for your personal journal use, but please do not use them to create items that you intend to sell.

120

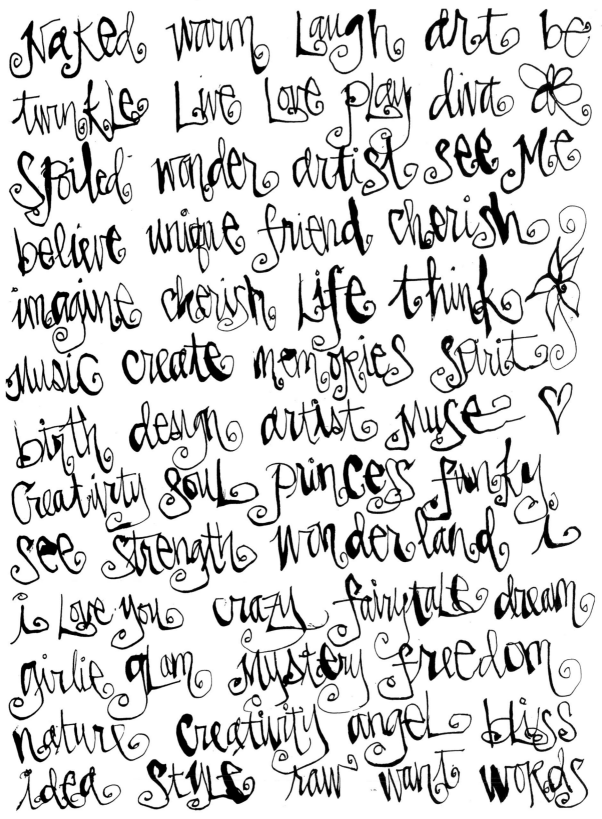

Naked warm Laugh art be twinkle Live Love play diva Spoiled wonder artist see Me believe unique friend cherish imagine cherish Life think music create memories spirit birth design artist Muse Creativity Soul princess funky see strength wonderland i i Love you crazy fairytale dream girlie glam Mystery freedom nature creativity angel bliss idea style raw want words

HAND-LETTERED WORDS

Use these ideas to explore doodling. Enlarge, photocopy, color, scan, print on iron-on transfers—the possibilities are endless!

INSPIRATION DOODLE IDEAS

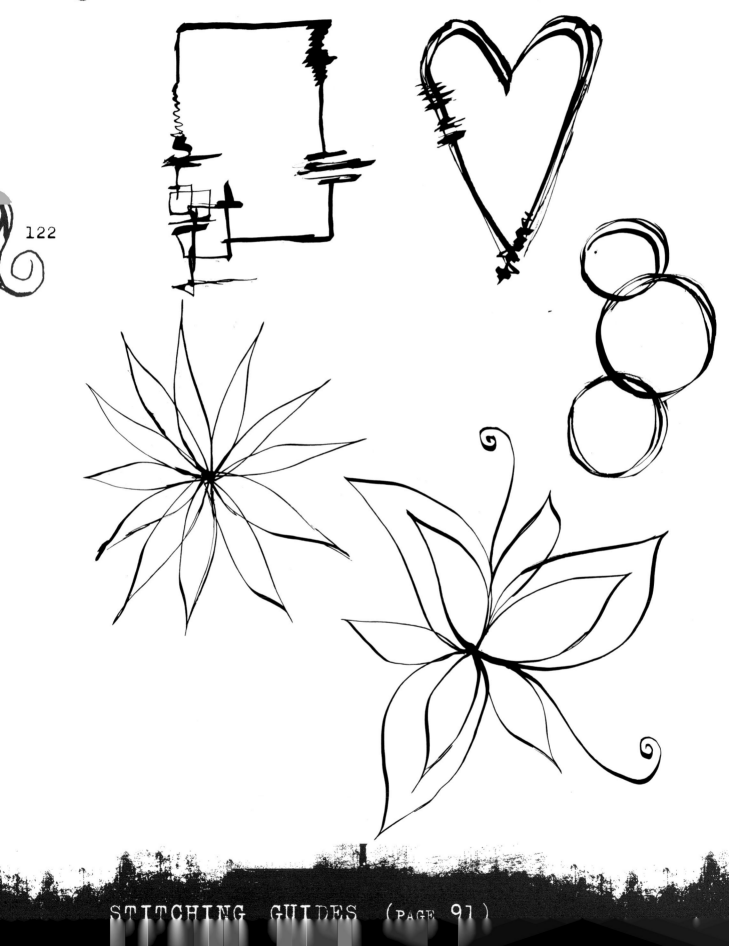

goodies

Use a copy of these patterns to practice free-form stitching with your sewing machine. See pages 91 and 92 for examples and instruction.

122

GIRLIE GLAM IMAGES

Here are some of my favorite stencil images. You can photocopy these and cut your own stencils from them, or alter them however you choose.

124

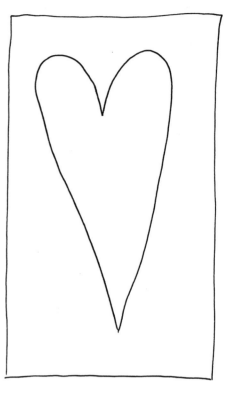

Use these black-and-white images to make your own photocopies and to experiment with color washes, or use them as layers in collage.

BLACK-AND-WHITE ART BACKGROUNDS

res●urces

Art Supplies

Crayola
crayons • Spider Writers • markers • glitter glue
www.crayola.com

Golden Artist Colors
acrylic paints • mediums
www.goldenpaints.com

June Tailor
inkjet fabric sheets • iron-on transfer sheets
www.junetailor.com

Pilot
parallel pens • oil-based gel pens • paint markers • V-pens
www.pilotpen.com

Ranger Industries, Inc.
Stickles dimensional glitter
www.rangerink.com

Inspirational Publications

The Art of Rebellion (Gingko Press, 2005)
by Christian Hundertmark

Celebrate Your Creative Self (North Light Books, 2003)
by Mary Todd Beam

Creative Stamping With Mixed Media Techniques
(North Light Books, 2003) *by Sherrill Kahn*

Don't Move the Muffin Tins (Burton Gallery, 1978)
by Bev Bos

Spilling Open (Villard, 2000) *by Sabrina Ward Harrison*
(www.sabrinwardharrison.com)

Craft books from the 1960s and the 1970s

Numerous works by SARK (www.planetsark.com)

Numerous works by Eric Carle (www.eric-carle.com)

Dover Publications books: Erté, art history, symbols

Art & Life zine by Teesha Moore (www.teeshamore.com)

Business 2.0 magazine (www.business2.com/b2/)

cloth paper scissors magazine
(www.quiltingarts.com/cpsmag/cpshome.html)

Communication Arts magazine
(www.commerce.commarts.com)

Dwell magazine (www.dwellmag.com)

Flaunt magazine (www.flaunt.com)

HOW magazine (www.howdesign.com)

metro.pop magazine (www.metrodotpop.com)

ReadyMade magazine (www.readymademag.com)

Somerset Studio magazine (www.somersetstudio.com)

W magazine (www.style.com/w/)

Wallpaper* magazine (www.wallpaper.com)

Wired magazine (www.wired.com)

Z!nk magazine (www.zinkmag.com)

Inspiring Artists

Nina Bagley (www.ninabagley.com)

Ann Baldwin (www.annbaldwin.com)

Lisa Engelbrecht (www.lisaengelbrecht.com)

Claudine Hellmuth (www.collageartist.com)

Aaron Kraten (www.aaronkratenart.com)

Teesha Moore (www.teeshamoore.com)

DJ Pettitt (www.djpettitt.com)

Lesley Riley (www.lalasland.com)

Further Inspiration

Asian Art Museum, San Francisco
*(a must-visit to experience symbols,
images and letterforms of ancient Asia)*
www.t26.com (online font foundry)

index

127

let creative playtime continue with these great titles from north light books

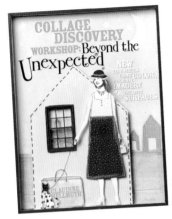

In a follow-up to her first workshop book, **Claudine Hellmuth** taps into a whole new level of creativity in Beyond the Unexpected. Inside you'll find original artwork and inventive ideas that show you how to personalize your own collage pieces using new techniques and interesting surfaces. In addition, the extensive gallery compiled by Claudine and other top collage artists will spark your imagination. Whether you're a beginner or a collage veteran, you'll enjoy this lovely book both as inspiration and as a practical guide.

ISBN 10: 1-58180-678-7
ISBN 13: 978-1-58180-678-6
paperback 128 pages 33267

Create a signature look with stamped images you carve yourself! **Gloria Page** introduces you to the world of carving and printing soft blocks to create great gifts, home décor items and personal apparel—all with a look uniquely yours. Detailed instructions on carving tools and techniques get you started. Then you'll learn to create 20 projects on paper, fabric and alternative surfaces, such as wood and polymer clay. Templates for recreating all stamp designs featured in the projects are included. Carving your own stamps gives you the freedom to use any image at any size and sets your work apart from the crowd. Discover the fulfillment that comes from printing your own images and start carving your stamps today!

ISBN 10: 1-58180-696-5
ISBN 13: 978-1-58180-696-0
paperback 128 pages 33355

Have you always wanted to dive into art journaling, but you're always stopped by what to put on the page? Finally, there is a book that comes to your rescue! Visual Chronicles is your no-fear guide to expressing your deepest self with words as art, and artful words. **Linda Woods & Karen Dinino** show you quick ways to chronicle your thoughts with painting, stamping, collaging and writing. Friendly projects like the Personal Palette and the Mini Prompt Journal make starting easy. You'll also find inspiration for experimenting with colors, shapes, ephemera, communicating styles, symbols and more!

ISBN 10: 1-58180-770-8
ISBN 13: 978-1-58180-770-7
paperback 128 pages 33442

More than 20 dramatic paint and stamping recipes combine sponging, glazing and masking techniques with stamped patterns for outstanding creations. **Sherrill Kahn** integrates traditional and nontraditional media in 13 step-by-step projects. Manipulate, decorate and combine different materials to create mixed media gifts and art objects that are sure to impress even the most creative of your friends!

These and other fine North Light titles are available from your local art and craft retailer, bookstore or online supplier.

ISBN 10: 1-58180-347-8
ISBN 13: 978-1-58180-347-1
paperback 128 pages 32315